D1588733

Tynnwyd o Stoc
Withdrawn from stock

WREXHAM C.B.C LIBRARY	
LLYFRGELL B.S. WRECSAM	
C56 0000 0458 899	
HJ	13-Oct-2009
306.874	£9.99
ANF	WR

Grandparents

A Celebration

Edited by
Sarah Brown and Gil McNeil

EBURY
PRESS

1 3 5 7 9 10 8 6 4 2

Published in 2009 by Ebury Press, an imprint of Ebury Publishing
A Random House Group Company

Collection copyright © PiggyBankKids Projects 2009

Each contributor has asserted their right to be identified as the
author of their individual contribution in accordance with the
Copyright, Designs and Patents Act 1988

All rights reserved. No part of this publication may be reproduced,
stored in a retrieval system, or transmitted in any form or by any means,
electronic, mechanical, photocopying, recording or otherwise,
without the prior permission of the copyright owner

The Random House Group Limited Reg. No. 954009

Addresses for companies within the Random House Group
can be found at www.randomhouse.co.uk

A CIP catalogue record for this book is available from the British Library

The Random House Group Limited supports The Forest Stewardship
Council (FSC), the leading international forest certification organisation.
All our titles that are printed on Greenpeace approved FSC certified paper
carry the FSC logo. Our paper procurement policy can be found at
www.rbooks.co.uk/environment

Mixed Sources

Product group from well-managed
forests and other controlled sources
www.fsc.org Cert no. TT-COC-2139
© 1996 Forest Stewardship Council

Designed and set by seagulls.net

Printed in the UK by CPI Mackays, Chatham, ME5 8TD

ISBN 9780091930783

To buy books by your favourite authors and register for offers visit
www.rbooks.co.uk

Contents

Introduction

Most people who are lucky enough to have met their grandparents have wonderful memories of them when they were growing up. I am lucky enough to have known all four of my grandparents and have loving memories of them all, which I treasure.

Some of my strongest recollections are of my two grandmothers. My mum's mother was a gentle woman who had travelled the world with my grandfather (who was a real hero of mine) in the diplomatic service, acting as the hostess everywhere imaginable. But what I remember most are her fried chicken bucket nights when they had retired to Ealing, which was the biggest treat imaginable for me and my brothers. We would gather a mountain of food and eat ourselves stupid while talking non-stop – all of us at the same time. Through it all she would remain one of the calmest people. I wish she could see my lovely sons as she was wonderful with babies and small children.

My Scottish Gran was very different – she had stayed in Scotland all her life and had great trepidations about being too far from home. My dad's dad had served in

India during the war, and I'm sure that added to her fear of seeing the family fly the nest. So when my mum and dad took me and my young brothers to live in East Africa it must have felt dreadful to her; having all of us so far away. Telephones not being what they are today, we had just one phone call at Christmas time which centred around shouting, "happy Christmas! Can you hear me, is it a good line? Hello, hello, happy Christmas!" before the pre-booked time was up.

My Scottish Gran was terribly stern with us but cherished small rituals when we made our annual visit to stay with her and Grandad in their pebble-dashed house for a week every summer. Every year we had the same cup and plate kept for each of us, and the thrill of ice cream from the local van squirted directly into the serving bowl followed by an episode of *Crossroads* or *Dr Who* on the black and white television (truly a unique thing for us as we had no access to a TV back in East Africa). My dad would always take his dad out for a curry in Edinburgh; a tradition between them which we all knew was a vital part of their summer.

I feel lucky compared to Gordon, whose grandparents died before he ever got to know them, so he had to rely on his mum and dad's memories. The story he always remembers about his father's parents was that they had married on their own farm in Fife in Scotland. When we were planning to marry and thinking of a way to do this fairly quietly, Gordon recalled this piece of family history and we did the very same thing, marrying in our own dining room. Now whenever we have a family meal or guests over to our house in Fife I always remember our beautiful wedding day. We also have a picture drawn of his grandparents' Fife house in our home, reminding us of that connection that binds us over the generations, even though we never met.

Now that I am a mum of two small children, working with a children's charity and involved with a number of other charities and campaigns, and adapting to the various demands of life in No 10, I appreciate that my own mother is around from time to time to help out and bring us together for family occasions. My mum is definitely from the new generation of grandparents; busy and active, learning new things and always volunteering to help others, but also making sure they spend time with all their grandchildren.

There are an estimated fourteen million grandparents in the UK, and many of them help their sons or daughters with childcare. Recent figures suggest 70 per cent of families with babies and nearly half of those with toddlers rely on grandparent carers – and for single parents, younger and first-time mothers, grandparents form a particularly vital part of their support network. One per cent of children are actually looked after full-time by their grandparents, for all kinds of reasons. Grandparents are such a vital part of family life today, it's important we do more to recognise their contribution.

How we treat older people in society is so important, and says a lot about us as a country. It is not just the fact that we should all find ways to care for our elderly, protecting their homes and their health, but that we should appreciate them, learn from them and draw them closer to the next generation. Everyone has so much to gain from each other. That is why we have included contributions in this collection from some of the experts running charities, associations and organisations committed to supporting older people.

This anthology contains witty, wry and often touching observations about being a grandparent, alongside moving and heartwarming memories of much-loved grandparents, together with some just plain laugh-out-loud stuff. But we have also included some more challenging contributions; Paul Dacre reminds us of how much we gain from bringing older generations closer to the heart of our families, and how much we risk losing if that link between the generations is broken, and Richard Eyre shares his experience of a difficult grandparent and the shadow they can cast across the generations.

Families today need flexibility and options, never more so than in these tough economic times. And we can all play our part – from the government to individual communities – to help provide for the dignity of our elderly, so they have the quality of life they deserve. As times move on, with more mums out at work, grandparents are going to play an even bigger part in our children's lives. As carers when they are very small, and as all important role models as they begin to grow into young adults.

That is why PiggyBankKids, the charity I set up in 2002 to help babies and children, leapt at the chance to support a project called Granny School when it was presented to the Trustees for funding. Through the Jennifer Brown Research Fund we support new community health projects run by midwives, nurses and other health professionals, who have ideas from their own daily working lives that might improve the care and provision for mothers, young babies and children.

Currently offered as part of a pilot project in Fife at the Queen Margaret Hospital in Dunfermline and the Forth Park Hospital in Kirkcaldy, Granny School offers refresher classes to first time grandmas. The inspiration of a Fife community midwife Carol Murray, every Granny School class has been oversubscribed and there is clearly a huge demand all over the UK for this kind of service.

Granny School is not about teaching grannies what to do, because for the most part they've got more to teach us. It's about them catching up on the things that have changed since they brought up their children. The classes offer up-to-date information about the care of new babies, toddlers and beyond, up to four years old, and so far they've been a raving success.

Children really matter to us at PiggyBankKids and by buying this book you are really showing how much they matter to you too. I know that many grandparents across Britain share our focus on wanting the best start in life for all children – not just their own precious grandchildren. As well as supporting PiggyBankKids' projects like the Granny School and similar projects providing help to some of the most vulnerable mums in our communities, the proceeds from the sale of the book will support the research at the Jennifer Brown Research Laboratory, where our talented and dedicated team of scientists are advancing pioneering research making real progress towards resolving some of the life-threatening complications that can arise during pregnancy.

The charity also supports with its Small Grants programme and Sharing Skills team a number of partnerships with charities supporting older children, ranging from mentoring to sports provision to cancer care. So thank you so much for buying this book and helping us to raise funds to support all our projects. I'd also like to thank Gil McNeil, my co-editor and Director of PiggyBankKids, and everyone at Ebury and PiggyBankKids for all their hard work. Most of all I would like to thank all our wonderful writers who have so generously agreed to contribute their work for free. And of course last, but not least, thanks to all our grandparents.

Sarah Brown
PiggyBankKids

Joan Bakewell

My granddad was tall, very tall to a small child. And he had great plate-sized hands. They were rough to the touch, because he was a cooper, a man who made barrels for Ardwick brewery in Manchester, so he worked with wood every day, shaping and shaving it. They say he could make a barrel to hold an exact quantity of beer, entirely by eye, without the use of measures or calculations. That was his pride, his pride in his craft.

He brought his skill home with him to a small shed in the garden that ran down to the railway line. Here we children used to hang over the railings waving at the steam engines as they roared by in the cutting below us. Sometimes, dimly, we could see a passenger waving back. When we got bored waiting for trains we would ask to be allowed into Granddad's shed. It was a long low timber building painted black, with a creosoted roof to keep the rain out. That was black too. He had to stoop his tall frame to get in. It was clearly a place of serious work. When the others got bored and turned to skipping ropes and hopscotch, I lingered. I came to love it – his place and, for a short while, shared with me.

Inside there was a circular black stove with a round metal lid you could lift off with a metal handle revealing the glowing coals within. He would stoke it up with some more coals in a small black shovel. Coal was plentiful. This was Lancashire and every home had a coal-hole, a coal shed or simply a heap stacked against a back wall. Granddad's stove had a chimney that stood free of the wall and pierced the low roof, sending smoke billowing out into the garden and sometimes onto the clean washing on the line. There had to be a stove because there was no other heating, no electricity and no light. I loved warming my hands, holding them out towards its black bulk. I was warned to be careful not to touch it as I would burn myself. That was but one hazard. There were plenty of others.

Granddad used the shed to make things. At one side were chunks of wood, sometimes as big as planks, leaning in a ramshackle heap ready for use. And along the wall under the four-paned window was Granddad's workbench, with planes, chisels and a bewildering spread of mysterious woodworking tools kept sharp and at the ready. I was warned they would cut and I was not to meddle. But it didn't stop me. I would be judge of my own danger. I didn't need grown-ups interfering.

The days I enjoyed most were when he was engaged in making something I could recognise: a stool, a table, a box. I loved the concentration he brought to his skill, not the intense concentration needed for something that was difficult, but the familiar concentration needed for something that was as familiar as getting dressed, and that had to be done in the correct order. He neither hurried nor loitered. He would whistle, a strange strained sound that came from wrapping his top lip over the bottom. It was a sharp, sour noise that indicated concentration rather than any love of music. I would watch as he planed the wood, great golden curls of shavings spinning out and falling to the floor where they would pile up, fragrant strands rising in weightless heaps until, to me at the age of six, they would reach almost waist high. I suppose he must have known that the rising tide of shavings lapping so close to the black stove was a fire hazard. But he never warned me, or seemed to take notice. The drifts would collect in corners and beneath his bench. There were cobwebs there, too, and spiders and dead flies. But I would brave their terrors to scoop up the discarded shavings and plunge my nose into their rich sappy smell. Before we packed up for the day he would brush down my dress with his huge brusque hands so that my mother wouldn't complain at the mess.

He would choose what to make from the clues within each piece of wood. So items emerged at random. It was no good my granny saying 'Mrs Beesley would like a bedside table'; Mrs Beesley would have to wait. The moment would come, no doubt, when the right wood arrived, but he would make no effort, service no orders, comply with no birthday requests. The making was all.

I am not sure where this ready supply of wood came from. I suspected in my sceptical teenage years that he was nicking it from the brewery. But the explanation is probably simpler: discarded wood, odd off-cuts and rejects were, I imagine, simply put out as waste and he made good use of them. That's why he had to accommodate such unconventional shapes.

My granddad lived to be ninety and died in an old people's home mourned by the second wife he had married at the age of eighty-four. I still have two stools made by him: they stand less than two foot tall and have legs that don't match. How I came by them I can't remember. I suppose they were a trade-off in those extended legacies that chase family objects down the decades. At one time they had been painted gloss white by someone impressed by Scandinavian lightness of style. By the time they reached me they were chipped and dirty. In the normal course of housekeeping I would have thrown them away. Except for the shed. I kept them in memory of the shed.

I sent them off to one of those places where they dip painted furniture in tanks of powerful liquid that eats back to the naked wood. The stools came back dull, almost grey. The zest had gone out of them. But a little teak oil has brought them back to life. They wobble a good deal, legs fall off and have on occasion let casual users down onto the carpet. But they are with me still, incongruous objects in a study of books and papers. Sometimes they support a pot of flowers. But mostly they stand alone, reminding me of golden wood shavings in a time of childhood.

Joan Bakewell has been a broadcaster on radio and television for over thirty years. She is also a print journalist, a novelist and, since November 2008, the government-appointed Voice of Older People.

Think of Your Granddad as Google

Trevor Beattie

*In honour and memory of my wonderful
grandparents, Joseph and Ellen Page.*

Think of your granddad as Google. It'll help explain his behaviour. He does what he does and says what he thinks for one very important reason: because he can.

When you're fifteen, you think you know everything. That no one can tell you what to do, what to say or how to behave. When you're eighty-five, you genuinely *do* know everything. And try as they might, no one can tell you what to do, what to say or how to behave.

Is it any wonder then, that the unlikely bond between teenagers and grandparents is so strong? Just at the moment you feel your parents don't *understand* you, you discover that your grandparents absolutely do. And no one does rebel with (or without) a cause better than your grandparents. They know, you know.

Had we had such a highfalutin' thing as a search engine back when I was a surly, arty fifteen-year-old Brummie know-all with a chip on each shoulder, my granddad would have been Google incarnate. Well, in cardie and slippers, at least.

The important differentiator however, is that grandparents don't just know *what*, they know *why*. And how it affected them. They offer wisdom, not just facts. And the wisdom of life experience is the most valuable commodity in the world.

It's one thing to read a screen full of cold facts about the First World War. It's quite another to have had a conversation with someone who survived a gas attack in the rat-infested flooded trenches of Ypres in 1917, before he'd even celebrated his twenty-first birthday. (I have his medals on the table before me as I write this.) Try telling Granddad Page he couldn't have an extra chocolate biscuit with his cuppa...

And proud as you may be of your Latest Flame, I'm afraid you'd find your fling flung into insignificance alongside a couple who spent half a century alongside one another though thick and thin, war and peace. From Kaiser Bill to Batman. That was my gran and granddad.

There's no shortcut to what our grandparents possess. But the simple joy for us is their desire and eagerness to spread the wisdom around. So don't wait to be asked. Fill your boots. They have time. Though sadly, not enough of it. If you're lucky enough to still have grand-parents, you are blessed indeed. So make the most of it. Stop 'visiting' websites and visit the Real Thing. Now.

Engage them. Question them. Listen to them. Chat. With mouth not mouse. Learn. Above all, enjoy what is by definition one of the shortest yet most vital of all human relationships: grandchild and grandparent. You'll find they really are the fountain of all knowledge.

Extremely human search engines. Click with them. Stick with them. With any luck, one day you'll be them.

Trevor Beattie is a founding partner of BMB Advertising, London.

Sir Ian Blair

I only met one of my grandparents, my mother's mother, named May but affectionately and accurately known as Spud. My principal memory of her – and she died when I was twenty-one so I saw a lot of her – is that she never complained. She was of a generation that saw plenty of hardship. She lived through two world wars. She lost her husband very early, during the Depression, when his business went bust and she lost almost everything.

She would live with one of her daughters for six months at a time. She was always jolly – or seemed to be to me – and she always had time. She was very comforting and smelled of a mixture of lavender and peppermint.

I am not sure the arrangement suited my parents quite as well as it suited her but, again, they were also of a generation that didn't complain.

The quality of just getting on with things, of looking on the bright side, of not looking for scapegoats, of being unflinching in the face of adversity is something from which I learned and which I will always admire. I just wish those qualities were more broadly evident today than they were when she was alive.

Sir Ian Blair was the 24th Commissioner of the Metropolitan Police from 2005 until the end of 2008. He was a police officer for more than 34 years and commanded the Met through the London bombings of July 2005.

Patti Boulaye

My grandmother, whom we called Nne Kamba (great-mother) did not survive the Biafran war and genocide but before the war, my holiday visits to her home in the village, are my fondest childhood memories. Nne Kamba did not like the hustle and bustle of life in the busy cities in Nigeria and preferred her simple lifestyle in the village.

The village was made up of fifteen or twenty thatched roofed mud huts. Nne Kamba had the largest and most modern, with white walls, a large veranda, four rooms to sleep in, a living area for entertaining guests, an outside kitchen and a pit toilet about ten metres into the forest at the back.

To get to the village we had to travel for hours, leaving the city at 6 a.m. and we would arrive before dark, having travelled through towns with hawkers literally attacking the cars as they tried to sell their goods. These could be anything from sweets or clothing to vegetables and we made these stops about nine or ten times before arriving at the river by the town. We would then board three canoes that looked like they would sink under the weight of all our cases and big bunches of plantain (my favourite vegetable) and other things we bought during the journey for grandmother. The edges of the canoes were dangerously only two inches above the water level, which made it feel as if you were sitting in the river. It was great fun to run our fingers over the water as the canoes slid along with the fishermen's paddles skilfully causing gentle waves. Then the scary stories would start about crocodiles and snakes and other creatures that live in the river and the forest. After about thirty minutes we would arrive at a clearing in the forest where a group of people would be waiting to carry our belongings about a mile into the forest to Grandmother's village.

It was easier as a child to use pit toilets; I tried it recently on a trip to Africa to open a clinic. I can't imagine why I have fond memories of holidays in the village, perhaps it was the dances and stories by the campfires or maybe the singing on the way to fetch the water from the river at 5.30 a.m. or the smell of fried plantain and fresh fish barbecue on an open fire after the spectacularly colourful fishing festivals.

I am so glad Nne Kamba did not like living in the busy towns. I wonder what my grandchildren would remember about me.

As I was growing up, I always wanted a family of six children and that is exactly what I got, our daughter and son and four stepdaughters, resulting so far in eight grandchildren.

Being a stepgrandmother is fantastic, especially when the grandchildren come up with lines that make you laugh every time you remember them and you also realise that sometimes their young minds hear and see things differently from the rest of us. They are funny without meaning to be and they don't only surprise you, they are always entertaining.

My eight stepgrandchildren have eight different characters. One of them, William, at the age of four came home one day from school where the teacher had been trying to find out from the children whether their parents were Catholics or Protestants for the purpose of first holy communion. William came home and shouted out, 'Mum, are we Catholics or Vegetarians?'

One of my other grandchildren, Beans, aged ten, (who is a young actor and attends Westminster Abbey Choir School) was asked to say grace during the family Christmas dinner. We were delighted at his enthusiasm, but his grace was short. 'Bless this bunch as they munch their lunch' he blurted out quickly and in all seriousness.

Patti Boulaye is a singer/songwriter, an actress and painter and is a fellow of the Royal Society of Art. She was a member of the Creative Team of HM the Queen's Golden Jubilee Celebrations.

Christopher Brookmyre

My late gran, Annie Dougan, deserves more blame for the kind of humour found in my work than most people might assume. One story she was fond of re-telling related an occasion when she happened to be visiting relatives on the other side of my hometown, Barrhead, and popped into a newspaper shop that she only occasionally frequented. As my gran had not been in for some weeks, the wee woman behind the counter seized upon the opportunity to bring her up to date with the latest news, which typically comprised a litany of death.

'You know Moira McGhee?' the proprietor inquired.

'Aye.'

'She died. Cancer. And you know Michael Gallagher?'

'Aye.'

'He died. Heart attack. And you know Vera Kelly that married Tommy Reilly?'

'Aye.'

'She died. Stroke.'

And so on, until, my gran decided to retaliate by adding: 'Terrible, aye. And I see the Pope died too.'

To which the wee woman gave the reply that so tickled my gran, and which contains the quintessence of the parochial mindset:

'Aye, but he never bought his paper fae us.'

Christopher Brookmyre is the author of thirteen novels, including Attack of the Unsinkable Rubber Ducks, A Snowball in Hell *and* Pandaemonium.

Fiona Bruce

Grandpa was a firm fixture in our lives. For most of my childhood, we used to descend on him for the summer weeks at his house by the sea in Margate. It never occurred to me that he might mind that his usually peaceful house was invaded by three noisy kids and my mother – if he did, he never showed any sign of it. We lived abroad and only saw him at Christmas and during the long summer holidays. He was a gentle soul, unfailingly kind, long widowed, who'd taught himself to cook and look after his house. He always made fudge for us, a sticky, incredibly sugary, tooth-rotting confection, which I loved.

His driving was a source of constant amusement to me and my two brothers. His glasses were thick and smeary and I wondered how he could see through them as he peered over the steering wheel. He drove at a steady twenty miles per hour, never faster, and wherever he went a long line of cars would form behind him, occasionally honking their frustration at being held up by Grandpa's snail-like progress. My brothers and I would sit in the back, shaking with laughter as Grandpa drove on, oblivious to everyone else on the road.

He was wonderfully forgetful. Once he drove up his steep driveway with Sheba, his enormous black Newfoundland dog, sitting upright on the back seat, drooling over the passenger seat in front. Grandpa switched the engine off, got out, adjusted his virtually opaque glasses and went inside the house. I suddenly heard my mother shouting. I raced to the front window and saw Grandpa's car rolling back down the driveway, picking up speed as it went. It veered backwards across the road and mounted the kerb of the pavement opposite before coming to a gentle stop against a lamp post. He'd forgotten to put the handbrake on. I can still see Sheba now, sitting in the back seat, just visible as the car rolled down the hill, quite unconcerned as the cars on the road swerved around her.

Fiona Bruce presents BBC News *and* Antiques Roadshow *on BBC1 as well as numerous documentary series. She has been a journalist for over twenty years and has won many awards for her work.*

From 'The Life and Times of the Thunderbolt Kid'
Bill Bryson

My grandfather was a rural route mailman by trade, but he owned a small farm on the edge of town. He rented out the land to other farmers, except for three or four acres that he kept for orchards and vegetables. The property included a big red barn and what seemed to me like huge lawns on all sides. The back of the house was dominated by an immense oak tree with a white bench encircling it. It seemed always to have a private breeze running through its upper branches. It was the coolest spot in a hundred miles. This is where you sat to shuck peas or trim green beans or turn a handle to make ice cream at the tranquil, suppertime end of the day.

I spent a lot of time following my grandfather around. He seemed to like the company. We got along very well. My grandfather was a quiet man, but always happy to explain what he was doing and glad to have someone who could pass him an oil can or a screwdriver. His name was

Pitt Foss Bryson, which I thought was the best name ever. He was the nicest man in the world after Ernie Banks.

He was always rebuilding something – a lawnmower or washing machine; something with fan belts and blades and lots of swiftly whirring parts – and always cutting himself fairly spectacularly. At some point, he would fire the thing up, reach in to make an adjustment and almost immediately go, 'Dang!' and pull out a bloody, slightly shredded hand. He would hold it up before him for some time, wiggling the fingers, as if he didn't quite recognise it.

'I can't see without my glasses,' he would say to me at length. 'How many fingers have I got here?'

'Five, Grandpa.'

'Well, *that's* good,' he'd say. 'Thought I might have lost one.' Then he'd go off to find a bandage or a piece of rag.

The other thing I did a lot was watch TV. My grandparents had the best chair for watching television – a beige leatherette recliner that was part fairground ride, part captain seat from a spaceship, and all comfort. It was a thing of sublime beauty and utility. When you pulled the lever you were thrust flung – into deep recline mode. It was nearly impossible to get up again, but it didn't matter because you were so sublimely comfortable that you didn't want to move. You just lay there and watched the TV through splayed feet.

My grandparents could get seven stations on their set – we could only get three in Des Moines – but only by turning the roof aerial, which was manipulated by means of a crank on the outside back wall of the house. So if you wanted to watch, say, KTVO from Ottumwa, my grandfather had to go out and turn the crank slightly one way, and if you wanted WOC from the Quad Cities he turned it another, and KWWI in Waterloo another way still, in each case responding to instructions shouted through a window. If it was windy or there was a lot of solar activity, he sometimes had to go out eight or nine times during a programme. If it was one of my grandmother's treasured shows, like *As the World Turns* or *Queen for a Day*, he generally just stayed out there in case an aeroplane flew over and made everything lapse into distressing waviness at a critical moment. He was the most patient man that ever lived.

Bill Bryson is a bestselling author and broadcaster.

Jane
Glynis Burrough

Winner of the Good Housekeeping *readers' competition.*

My grandmother Jane was a spark that nobody could extinguish. Not surprisingly she started a few fires along the way. Born in South Shields in 1904, she was of the same generation as Catherine Cookson. She was so full of love and life and fun, with an open heart and an open purse, she always gave without asking for or expecting anything in return.

She always went out 'dressed' – a natty little hat raked at a devilish angle, matching gloves and a pretty scarf, and of course her most important accessory: a cigarette. She had always been a very bad example for the anti-smoking lobby; she smoked from the age of fourteen until two years before her death at the age of ninety-eight. Despite her constant intake of nicotine she always looked years younger than she was, this mostly due to her beautiful skin, which, she claimed, was due to her old favourite – Pond's Cold Cream.

I spent my summer holidays with Grandma. She'd take the hems up on my dresses and put ribbons in my hair. We'd go shopping in Newcastle and have lunch in Fenwick's department store where we'd be served by a waitress in a black dress and a frilly hat. Grandma taught me to knit and crochet, to cook, to look after plants, how to bath budgies and teach them to talk. We'd play endless Scrabble and card games and she would let me stay up to watch *Sunday Night at the London Palladium*. I could read all my mother and auntie's childhood books which Grandma had never thrown away. But my favourite time with Grandma was when she told me the stories of her life.

She was always one of the first to try anything. At a time when the ladies' fashion was to have long hair, Grandma saw a picture of an Eton Crop in a magazine and took the plunge. She was one of the first to dance the Charleston and even won prizes for it, dancing with the man who had taught her – my grandfather – who had learned the dance in New York.

Grandma loved swimming and also loved knitting, but the two didn't mix. She knitted herself a bathing suit and went swimming, emerging from the waves with the suit stretched to her ankles. Another first – flashing.

Grandma adored dancing but her father was strict. She had to be home by 8 p.m., which she was, but would then wait until he had gone to the pub before climbing out of the window and returning to the dance halls.

At twenty-one she decided to train as a mental-health nurse in Epsom. She worked with children, for whom she had a great affinity, but unfortunately never completed her training due to her mother 'persuading' her to come home. This she greatly regretted, but later in life was delighted when one of her daughters became a nurse. Her next job was in Crofton's, the local department store. She was regularly sacked by Mr Crofton for her cheek but was always reinstated by the end of the day.

She had many admirers but Granddad was determined to make her his. He'd fallen for her at first sight and told her she was going to marry him. She laughed. Then one day in 1928 he came into Crofton's with a marriage licence and said, 'How about it?' She said she thought it would be a shame to waste the licence fee so off they went to get married. Nobody in the family knew until they got home at teatime. After ascertaining that Grandma was not pregnant, Granddad was welcomed into the family. They were together until his death sixty-three years later.

Not long after my mother was born, Granddad became seriously ill – almost paralysed and blind. Grandma nursed her young baby and her husband while letting rooms to holidaymakers to make ends meet. With great courage Granddad finally made it back to work (he said it was the only thing for which he could thank Hitler – Great Britain was desperate for seamen).

In 1937, after the sudden death of her mother, Grandma gave up her own home to look after her father, brothers and sisters. At that time she herself had been diagnosed with thyroid disease but refused treatment. She said she didn't have time to be ill, she had a family to look after.

At the age of thirty-nine after a gap of fourteen years, Grandma's second child was born just after the D-Day landings. Granddad was at sea on the convoys to Archangel, Russia. He was a little surprised to receive a telegram telling him he was again a father. He hadn't known Grandma was pregnant, as her letters had not got through. He didn't see his new daughter until she was six months old.

Though pregnant, Grandma had been an ARP warden and often told the story of an Australian soldier pushing her under a table in the ARP headquarters just before a bomb fell on the house next door. She emerged covered in soot but unharmed.

Grandma didn't have a garden but made the most of her windowsills by filling them with beautiful plants. She talked to them every day and watered them with tea. They loved her dearly and blossomed with pleasure.

Grandma loved animals and was a regular rescuer – from Billy the goldfish who received a drop of whisky and mouth-to-mouth resuscitation after having been found outside of his bowl, to Limpy the canary with a broken leg for whom she made a special perch so that he could still swing on one leg – no animal was left unloved.

Her budgies would perch on the corner of her spectacles and chat to her as she did her crossword. They often developed a yellowish tinge due to the constant stream of cigarette smoke. In later years, when she lived with my parents, Grandma often set fire to my mother's cat. So engrossed in her crossword, she would forget the burning cigarette in her fingers until the ashy end collapsed and ignited the dozing cat on her knee.

At seventy, Grandma was still climbing out of windows. Carrying a basket of wet laundry to be hung out on a clothesline at the back of the building (there was no back door), she had climbed on a chair, over a dressing table, through a window and down a stepladder. On the return journey she lost her balance due to the loss of laundry counterbalance and fractured a rib.

At eighty-five she disappeared down an open manhole while on her way to Bingo with Granddad. When he eventually found her, he asked cheekily what she was doing down the manhole. She quipped she was just trying it out for size before she met her maker. It took four people to get her out. Luckily she had only cut her finger.

As she got older, dear Grandma could out-rival any Mrs Malaprop. At times it was quite charming; candelabras became 'candle-bras', but at other times it was hilarious – when I was sixteen she announced to my new boyfriend that her sister Dora had been a magnificent penis (she meant pianist).

She always said she was determined to outlive the Queen Mother but didn't quite make it. Just before her death at the age of ninety-eight, she still claimed to go out dancing every night but alas it was in her dreams – or so we assumed – we never did check the windows.

I wish she could have stayed for ever.

Glynis Burrough was born Glynis Witts in South Shields in 1956. At the age of twenty-two she left the UK to explore the world and over a period of thirty years lived in Bahrain, Argentina, Spain and Switzerland. She now lives in south-west France with her husband, dog, and two cats.

Tanya Byron

Both my grandmothers were women ahead of their time. They had their children in the 1930s and brought them up as single mothers. They went out to work and made sure their children – my parents – had a good home and education despite the very little money available to them.

My grandmother's were both women of immense style and dignity who had lived through turbulent times. Cynthia Corbett – my maternal grandmother – was born and lived in India where her father worked on the railways. My mother was born in Calcutta in 1937 but when she was a young girl they all had to leave suddenly for England due to the rising tensions and hostilities in a country defining its independence. My grandmother spent a lot of her life feeling angry.

My father's mother, Carmen Blanck Sichel, was a feisty German Jewess from a wealthy family. She fled Germany not long after Kristallnacht in 1938 and came to Britain with her baby son. She had lost both her parents in concentration camps and was plagued by depression for most of her life.

I loved both these women and now as an adult I am so proud of who they were and what they achieved in times of adversity. I am especially proud of them because they survived and succeeded as single mothers at a time when such women were shunned by society and seen as failures in marriage.

Both my grandmothers were difficult women as they became older – demanding and fractious. However they also both retained their most dry and wicked sense of humour and were always very loving to both myself and my sister Katrina. Indeed, although neither of them would ever have defined themselves as feminists, they imbued in us both a sense that anything is possible if you show courage and commitment.

I think back to their lives and their struggles and I wonder how they coped. Interestingly I then remember that both of them had little phrases that they would tell Katrina and myself as we were growing up. These phrases were written in every birthday card and as I look at them now, seem to represent what both these women instinctively knew they needed to hold on to in order to get through life.

My grandmother Cynthia – a woman robbed of her country of birth and her cultural identity – feisty, funny but so often angry, would say:

Each day's a new beginning
So start it with a smile.
Enjoy the art of giving
The things that are worthwhile,
Like loving and forgiving
And having time to spare
To make somebody happy
By showing that you care.

My grandmother Carmen – a women who by virtue of her religion was left without parents, a home, an identity – feisty, funny but so often sad, would say:

Turn your stumbling blocks into your stepping-stones.

I am so proud of my grandmothers – for all they were, for all they achieved and for all they overcame. I am indebted to them both for raising the two incredible people who became my wonderful parents. I often miss them and wish they could have met my children – their great-grandchildren. I also wonder whether they would have been proud of me; I hope so.

Professor Tanya Byron is a Consultant Clinical Psychologist, broadcaster, journalist, author and government advisor.

Andrew Calder

It is one of my great regrets that none of my four grand-parents were alive at the time I was born and so I never knew any of them, nor was I able to enjoy the love I know they would have lavished on me. On the other hand, for that very reason I probably have a heightened appreciation of what my parents and those of my wife meant to our children. And now that we have two lovely little granddaughters of our own we see the other side of the coin: the pure delight they bring to our lives as we watch them grow and develop their unique personalities.

Having spent my entire professional career caring for mothers as they experience pregnancy and childbirth, I have a special awareness of the vital importance of fami-lies. Family members are all able to support each other in a huge number of different ways. Not only can the older members support and encourage the younger ones; it can often happen in the opposite direction, even when the young are very young. Such support is at its most important in times of hardship and sorrow. It is the direct result of the joys and happiness we share in the good times.

Grandparents are often the marvellous extra ingredient in the family, not least because of their wisdom and experience but because they may have more time to devote to their grandchildren while their parents are hard pressed.

I once heard it said that the secret of success in life is to choose the right grandparents – not easy to do, but we certainly carry their genes and we should cherish them for those and all the other things they have brought us – their love, guidance and encouragement.

Andrew Calder is Professor of Obstetrics and Gynaecology at the University of Edinburgh and Consultant in these disciplines at the Royal Infirmary of Edinburgh. His principal clinical and research focus is on the biological mechanisms of pregnancy, labour and delivery. He is the founding director of the Jennifer Brown Research Laboratory, funded by PiggyBankKids, which aims to improve understanding of the causes and consequences of low birth weight in order to reduce the incidence of stillbirth, neonatal death and long term handicap.

Love Frok Me

Stephanie Calman

My grandmother, Lizzie MacDonald, grew up in The Gorbals, the poorest part of Glasgow, in the early twentieth century. She won a medal for being the top student in her school, but had to leave at thirteen to go to work. She escaped her background by marrying my grandfather, who worked in a bank. He got promoted and they lived comfortably, but she was never able to realise her potential. She could play anything on the piano by ear, and loved playing bridge and going to the theatre, while my grandfather was mad about golf, which she loathed. Once, coerced into playing in a ladies' tournament and bored witless, she teed up at the green, bent down to swing, then said as she turned to the spectators,

'I expect you can see my drawers!'

Her joke did not go down well.

She also, according to my mother, used to insert inappropriate asides into the books she read them at bedtime. For example, while reading from *The Three Musketeers* she would say something like,

"'Then I shall ride with you!' cried D'Artagnan, as he leapt astride his horse, pausing only to vomit into a small hand bowl.'"

And my mother and aunt would say, 'He didn't *really*?!' to which my grandmother would reply, 'Just wanted to make sure you were paying attention.'

Once my mother had moved to London, Granny wrote often, and always signed off *'Love from me'*. One day she typed *'Love frok me'* by mistake, and kept it on like a kind of trademark. That one letter on the keyboard said so much about her refusal to bow completely to convention, and showed that inside the respectable bank manager's wife the subversive, original free spirit was still alive and kicking.

Stephanie Calman is a writer and broadcaster and the creator of www.badmothersclub.com. Her column 'Happy Families' appears in the Daily Telegraph. *Her latest book is* How (Not) to Murder Your Mother *and she is still married to author Peter Grimsdale, with whom she has two children.*

Jimmy Carr

My first memory of my maternal grandfather is of his dying. Which was typical of him. Not actually dying, you understand, but being in a state of 'dying'. I think it might be an Irish Catholic thing.

He was dying the entire time I knew him, only eventually making good on the promise a good twenty years later.

The first thing I can remember of my grandfather was meeting him after a major operation. He wasn't expected to pull through (he did, of course). Four-year-old me was ushered into a darkened room to say goodbye. I didn't have anything to say but sensed an awkward silence so filled it with some recently acquired information I mistakenly thought would be hugely comforting. I said 'We'll put flowers on your grave.' He laughed. It wasn't meant to be a joke. But a child pointing out the elephant in the room, the thing no one was talking about, was enough to make him crack a smile.

That was the beginning of our relationship. A relationship that consisted of little other than jokes.

My grandfather told all his grandchildren jokes. Jokes that were more like little riddles when we were infants.

> *What has four legs and says 'Boo'?*
> *A cow with a cold.*

> *What has four legs and says 'Aaaa'?*
> *A sheep with no lips.*

> *What's orange and sounds like a parrot?*
> *A carrot.*

And the one that's still my favorite:

> *Two cannibals are eating a clown. One says to the other,*
> *'Does this taste funny to you?'*

I, rather predictably, found them fascinating. And credited my grandfather with their creation.

In the years that followed after my first 'joke' with my grandfather, I visited my family in Ireland every summer and saw him often. We never got much beyond joking together. But the jokes did get better as I got older. Which is just as well as I wasn't told any of them just the once.

> *A man sees a farmer walking with a pig and notices that the animal has a wooden leg. Curious,*

he asks the farmer how the pig lost its limb. 'Well,' says the farmer, 'one night the wife and me were asleep when the pig spotted the house was on fire. It broke down the door, ran up the stairs and dragged me to safety. Then it went back in and carried out my wife. Then it went in a third time and rescued my four children. We'd all be dead if it weren't for this pig.'

'So did the pig get its leg burned in the fire?' asks the man.

'Oh, no,' says the farmer. 'But when you've got a pig like this, you don't eat it all at once.'

A man walks into a doctor's. 'Doctor, I'm suffering from silent gas emissions. All day at work, I have these silent gas emissions. Last night during a movie, I had ten silent gas emissions. On the way to your office, I had five silent gas emissions. And while sitting in your waiting room, I had three silent gas emissions. As a matter of fact, I've just had two more.'

The doctor replies, 'Well, the first thing we're going to do is check your hearing.'

Some of the jokes my grandfather told were 'Irish' jokes. Coming from an Irish Catholic family and growing up in the Home Counties of England does result in a fair amount of teasing. I always liked 'Irish' jokes. I like to think my grandfather wasn't just trying to make me laugh but teaching a valuable lesson: that you must be able to laugh at yourself. And also maybe passing on a sense of cultural identity.

Ireland's worst air disaster occurred early this morning when a small two-seater Cessna plane crashed into a cemetery. Irish search and rescue workers have recovered 1,826 bodies so far and expect that number to climb as digging continues.

An Irishman wanders into a library and says, 'Fish and chips, please'. The librarian says, 'I'm sorry, but this is a library.' The Irishman whispers, 'sorry, fish and chips, please.'

It's difficult for men, especially men of my grandfather's generation, to express emotion. It would have been nice for my grandfather to have told me that he loved me and that he hoped I loved him. But that is an awkward thing to say and it never happened. But what did happen was a lot of jokes.

A joke is a shorthand – it's telling someone that you like them without actually having to say it. That's what the joke really means.

Years after my grandfather's death I read somewhere

that a laugh is the shortest distance between two people. I rather like that.

When my grandfather finally died for real, someone told me this one at his wake:

An old woman is upset at her husband's funeral. 'You have him in a brown suit and I wanted him in a blue suit.'

The mortican says, 'We'll take care of it, madam,' and yells back, 'Ed, switch the heads on two and four!'

He would have laughed.

Jimmy Carr is a comedian, presenter, acrobat and gentleman. His first book, The Naked Jape, *examines the history of jokes and the psychology of joking. It's the sort of literature you might find in a downstairs loo.*

Recipe From My Grandmother

Georgina Chapman

WORCESTER PUDDING

Ingredients:

2 large eggs

4 oz butter

4 oz white caster sugar

4 oz white self-raising flour

½ pint milk

Directions:

Grease shallow baking dish (1 pint size). Set (fan) oven to 180 degrees.

Beat together butter and sugar until pale and creamy. Beat eggs and whisk into butter and sugar mix. Whisk until mixture is smooth. Fold in flour. Carefully add milk and mix gently.

Pour mixture into prepared baking dish and put in oven on middle shelf. Cook for approximately 25-30 minutes or until light brown on top and just firm to the touch.

Serve immediately with cream if desired.

Georgina Chapman is a British fashion designer and actress and the co-founder of fashion label Marchesa.

Reginald Ward: A Sip Of Tonic

Andrew Collins

If I write about my mum's father, Reginald Ward, it is not out of favouritism. He's simply the grandparent I feel I knew best out of the four – and the only one who called me 'Pidge', which was short for 'Pigeon'.

We were lucky enough to grow up with a full set on both sides: Nan and Pap Collins on my dad's, and Pap Reg and Nan Mabel on my mum's. All lived long lives and loomed as large and colourfully as any grandparent ought. Sweets, comics, workbenches, walks in the park and two very different kids of homemade pastry evoke the grandparental influence (the generous, savoury petticoat Nan Collins ran round the side of a roasting tin, and the neat, sugar-glazed crust on Nan Mabel's handed-down treacle tart recipe). Incidentally, in Northampton, 'pap' is the colloquial default for 'grandfather', and 'nan' for 'grandmother'. You should know this.

The big difference between the two sets was mobility: Pap Collins rode a scooter, but in the main he and Nan relied on lifts, legs or public transport. Meanwhile, Pap Reg could drive and had a car, which he drove well into his seventies. Of the two couples, Reg and Mabel were, relatively speaking, the 'posh' ones, in that they lived in a bungalow with a front garden, while the other nan and pap lived in a terrace looking out on the street. Reg was a toolmaker who had turned shop steward, which led him on the path to a full-time job working for the Amalgamated Engineering Union (later the Amalgamated Union of Engineering Workers). He came from working-class stock but since his dad was a clerk for London Midland and Scottish Railway, this made them, in Mum's words, 'upper crust' round Jimmy's End.

Pap Reg died in 2001, aged eighty-five, still active with the pressure group Pensioners' Voice. I wished he'd lived to see the book I wrote about my childhood, because he formed an important part. I recorded with wonder that he could remember stuff from as far back as the early 1920s, like the address where his headmistress lived (the corner of Forfar Street and Harlestone Road) and the specific Meccano set his parents bought him while off school with whooping cough aged six (the A1 set). This made him a lot like me. We bonded when I was a student finding my political feet in London. It dawned on me in that period of enlightenment that our nans and paps were really interesting people.

Reg, in particular, had hands-on experience of industry and collective bargaining. We found common ground in our views on workers' rights and government wrongs in the second half of the 1980s, a vital connection for the burgeoning undergraduate socialist. His first-ever job, aged fourteen, had been producing and assembling parts for model trains; I was already in my twenties and still in pampered education.

I'm glad I got to know Pap Reg while he was around, to value his generation's unique contribution and its hotline to the beginning of the century. He gave me my first sip of beer, when I was much too young to appreciate it, which he always called 'tonic', just as he always called me 'Pidge.' I raise a glass to him now.

Andrew Collins is a scriptwriter, journalist and broadcaster whose 1970s-set memoir Where Did It All Go Right? *is essentially a hymn to his family – and his grandparents.*

Mary Contini

I remember my Nonna just before she died. Eighty-five, widowed and wheelchair-bound but still sharp, strong, smartly dressed and hair blue-rinsed every Wednesday morning. I had married just the year before and she approved of my choice and was thrilled to hold Francesca, my new baby daughter.

When I was much younger I had spent much more time with her. She lived in Port Seton, a picturesque fishing village with my uncle and his family. Most Sundays saw me helping her prepare lunch: setting the table, sieving tomatoes, grating Parmigiano. She was a natural cook, preparing only Italian recipes she had learned when she was young; seasonal food closely linked to the fasting and feasting of the Catholic Calendar. Homemade pasta on Sundays with a thick, sweet tomato sugo; homemade chicken broth if we were poorly; fish on Fridays; baccalá on Good Friday, no meat during lent – no discussion!

My first visit to Italy was with Nonna, she returned to her family home in the south for months every summer. I, an innocent fourteen-year-old, miniskirted and naive, was introduced to my first taste of prosciutto, first sip of Chianti and first kiss with a lovely Italian boy... the latter only because he was gay and studying to be a priest – no discussion!

She taught me to play '*Scopa*,' the Italian card game, with her friends, groups of old folk who hung out in the bar in the *piazza*. Gambling was fine as long as you beat the men – no discussion!

During the last few years of her life, as she became ill and I pursued my life as a young career woman, I spent less and less time with her. She continued to cook every day and her afternoons found her sitting at her window, gazing out at life passing by, prayer book open and rosary beads in hand. She was quiet and peaceful, apparently content to be left alone.

She died, we wept and life went on. Francesca grew up, my own life took over and Nonna's picture gathered dust at the side of my bed.

It was not until twenty years later, when my own father died and it was Francesca's turn to leave home to study and work, that I started to think about Nonna again. It dawned on me that I knew little if anything about her. Though I had spent many happy times with her, she had never discussed things with me, her life, her views, her experiences.

She had never explained how it was she was Italian but lived in a Scottish fishing village and spoke English perfectly with a London accent. She never explained when she had been widowed or how. She never spoke to me in Italian.

It took me many years to piece together her story. She had been born in London in 1895, of two Italian immigrants from the Abruzzi region of Italy, poor shepherds who were driven to England with their family in order to survive.

She grew up in the slums of Little Italy, Saffron Hill; her father scraping a living in the streets making music with a barrel organ, a monkey dancing on top. When she was seven her mother died and her father and the rest of her five brothers were forced to return to the poverty in Italy they had tried to leave behind. They lived in a hovel of farm buildings with no running water or electricity and she spent most of her youth cooking and cleaning to care for her widowed father and orphaned brothers. She had to work on the land, herding sheep and making cheese.

When she blossomed into a beautiful young woman a second chance to start a new life came at nineteen when she fell in love with and married her first cousin Cesidio. Their first son died of fever aged three months, and then two other children were born, a daughter, Anna and a son, Giovanni, my father.

She never told me how her husband had been called up to fight with the Italian army when her son was just born or why, when he returned he left again to emigrate to join a cousin in Edinburgh. She never explained how she coped when he sent money over to her and asked her to follow him, alone with her two children, to a new life in Scotland.

She never discussed what she felt like when no sooner had they settled in a room at the back of a fish and chip shop in a fishing village outside Edinburgh then the First World War broke out and her young husband was called off to fight with the British in the Northern front. How did she manage to cope alone in a foreign country, expecting another child, left with a fledgling business to run and feed two children?

But she did manage. When her husband returned three years later she had not only survived but paid off debts, and made good friends among the Scottish women whose husbands were also at war.

When the Second World War broke out she was not so lucky. This time the Italians were the enemy. Who knows why she never spoke of her anguish and fear when, without warning, in the dark of night of the 20 June 1940, government officials came to her door and arrested her husband and two teenage sons at gunpoint. She never spoke of the terror and pain as she searched the city to find out what had happened. Not till the second week in July did she get news that he was missing and had probably drowned. Along with 446 other Italians, all men with similar stories and families left behind, he had gone down with the cruise ship, the *Arandora Star*, which was being used by the British government to transport 'dangerous aliens' to Canada. She never shared the anguish when she realised she would never see her husband again; she never screamed at her anger of why her loving, hardworking husband had been classed as a 'dangerous alien'. Anyone who knew him said he was a quiet kind man with not an ounce of malice in him.

She never told me what it felt like during the war years, her husband missing at sea; her eldest son imprisoned on the Isle of Man; her youngest son, a British citizen, fighting with the RAF in Africa against Mussolini's army. How could she talk about this?

Today, I am so proud of her and my grandfather. I regret deeply that I never talked with her while she was alive. I thought of her as an old lady, out of touch with my life. I loved her but I never knew her. Should I have tried harder? Oh yes – no discussion.

Mary Contini is a Director of the iconic Italian delicatessen, Valvona & Crolla, in Edinburgh. She writes about Italian food and her experiences of growing up in an Italian immigrant family. She campaigns avidly to improve children's diets but eats too much ice cream! She is married with two girls.

Double-decker Mummies
Jilly Cooper

I wrote this piece back in the late seventies for the Sunday Times *and although the reference to the Queen and Mrs Thatcher possibly becoming grandmothers in the near future does date it a bit, I don't feel our attitude to grannies has changed that much and I do hope you enjoy it.*

Of my grandparents, I remember my mother's mother best. A beauty even to the end, she had rose-petal skin, innocent blue eyes and swept-up white hair, with a rakish blond streak at the front from chain-smoking. She perfectly fitted Wordsworth's description of an old lady: 'Serene and bright, and lovely as a Lapland night.'

Most of her time was spent reading novels: Jane Austen, Thackeray, Mrs. Henry Wood, holding the book on top of a pair of combinations. If anyone came into the room, she would hastily whip the combinations over the book and pretend to be sewing.

Good works were not really her forte but, being a cler-gyman's wife, she made a great effort. On one occasion, my aunt surreptitiously added the dog's and cat's names to her prayer list, and the entire Mother's Union were exhorted in a ringing voice to pray for Raggety Bones and Mewkins.

Intensely gentle, a great giggler and a chronic pessimist (she would never admit to being anything better than 'fairly well, darling'), she was teased and yet adored by all her grandchildren. She in turn sent us fruit-cake and wrote us long illegible letters at school. My cousin, aged eight, remembers curling up in embarrass-ment when his form master deciphered one of them in front of the whole class: 'I saw Mummy today,' he read, then turning over two pages by mistake, 'she has a long black fluffy tail, and green eyes.'

Like the best grannies, she was a great character, as was one of my husband's grandmothers, who read *The Times* every day in asbestos gloves and, at the age of eighty-three, smashed the drawing room chandelier with her walking stick demonstrating how Arnold Palmer should have played an iron shot. Her funeral too was fitting. During the cremation service, the record got stuck on 'Abide Abide Abide with Me', which would have made her cackle with laughter. Afterwards everyone repaired to her house and had a rip-roaring party on Australian burgundy unearthed from the cellar.

Attitudes towards grandmothers vary from country to country of course. In France, the grandmère lives in the same house, ruling despotically over a vast family. The Eskimo shoves his granny out on the ice floe. The English tend to put her in a home, or a Tunbridge Wells boarding house, and forget her except for the occasional pilgrimage of avarice if she happens to be rich.

The young have been adulated in this country for so long that I suspect the pendulum is swinging back and the grandmother is about to become a cult figure. We live in such confused times that suddenly grandparents as a symbol of marital stability and old-world standards have become very attractive.

The Queen, for example, after a triumphant Jubilee year, is about to become a grandmother, so probably over the next few years will Mrs Thatcher, Shirley Williams, Antonia Fraser, even Brigitte Bardot.

For most of us the ideal grandmother is a cosy, twinkling-eyed Mrs Tiggywinkle figure and, fortunately for most women, the thrill of having grandchildren seems amply to compensate for a superficially ageing image. Can one be a grandmother and a *grande horizontale* at the same time, though? Certainly one can in fiction – there was a book called *The Love Habit* entirely devoted to the gallivantings of an erotomaniac granny.

The biggest excitement seems to be when one's daughter has her first baby: 'I never dreamt how overjoyed I'd feel,' said one young granny. 'As though I was having a baby of my own without the birth pains. I could never understand why people spoiled their grandchildren so much, but once it happens you hold this little thing in your arms and suddenly you're aware of immortality, of life growing on through you on a bigger scale. You have this incredible sense of the flow of time, of having one's own stake in eternity.'

Or, as my daughter said in a moment of lucidity, a granny is just a double-decker Mummy.

All blessings, however, are mixed blessings and having achieved the miracle of a grandchild, the grandmother's next problem is to keep her trap shut. 'You feel the baby is not being looked after exactly as you would wish,' said one. 'In my day we washed nappies and didn't automatically pick up a child when it started crying. But you bite your tongue off not to interfere.'

The wolf dressed up as a grandmother perhaps wasn't such a fairy tale. 'What big eyes you've got, Granny!'

'All the better to see where Mummy's going wrong in bringing you up, darling.'

Visits to grandparents, particularly when children are in the rough-housing stage, can be murder – all those footballs snapping the Regalia lilies, and sticky little hands stretching out for the Rockingham. Meal times are often a nightmare too.

'Why do all my grandchildren eat as though they're gardening?' said one granny. To which her grandchild, who was examining her wrinkles, replied: 'And why have you got a striped face, Granny?'

A grandmother, of course, is also a mother-in-law and unless she has a relaxed and affectionate relationship with her daughter-in-law, the grandchildren, inheriting their mother's animosity, will tend to prefer the maternal grandmother to the paternal one. I adored my paternal grandmother, but I was always in awe of her. I suspect it was because the tension and the desire to prove herself as a good wife and mother, that my mother displayed in my grandmother's presence, was transmitted to me even as a small baby.

Invariably there's rivalry between grandmothers, a sort of granny-mosity, not just larger hats at the christening but a very natural desire to be loved best. My children always get a kick on the ankles when they muddle Granny Brighton and Granny 'Orkshire on the telephone.

'I was staying with my daughter for the weekend,' admitted one granny, 'and the children made a terrific fuss of me, then suddenly my son-in-law's mother arrived and they were all over her. It's so undignified to sulk at my age.'

A grandmother also tends to prefer the eldest grandchild on both sides. She has known them longer and therefore better. Often when a second child is born and the limelight shifts from the first child, it turns to its grandparents for the extra spoiling and understanding it needs.

In fact, grandparents and grandchildren seem to

get on better left on their own. Two generations are company, three's a crowd. Just as granny's aware of the flow of time when her grandchild is born, grandchildren in turn are fascinated by their roots; it gives them a sense of belonging to hear anecdotes of the old days, of Uncle Willy's peccadilloes and how naughty Mummy and Daddy were when they were children.

Together they can revel in first and second childhoods and they do have the same enchanting tendency towards malapropisms. My son came back from a trip to Battle Abbey in July, saying he'd had a lovely time 'exploring a middle-aged castle'. Five minutes later my mother rang up. 'Wasn't it wonderful, darling, Virginia Woolf winning Wimbledon.'

Jilly Cooper is a journalist and the author of many number one bestselling novels, including Riders, Rivals, Polo *and* Wicked!. *Her non-fiction books include* Class *and* The Common Years. *She lives with her husband, two cats and a rescued greyhound in Gloucestershire. She was appointed OBE in the 2004 Queen's Birthday Honours List for her contribution to literature.*

Paul Dacre

For various reasons, neither I, nor my wife, really knew our grandparents. So I shall ask for your forbearance and write instead abut the woman who was 'grandma' in our home for many years: my wife's mother, Rose.

She was a Catholic shop assistant who fell in love with a postman who happened to be a Protestant – a sin for which she was summarily excommunicated by her priest. But then this was Liverpool in the late 1930s when religion was only marginally less important than life and death.

Rose and Charlie married and eventually were lucky enough to move to a newly-built council estate in Huyton on land bought from the neighbouring Lord Derby, who insisted that all homes built on what had been his estate should be in the Georgian style and have front and back gardens.

Thus it was in a tiny Georgian-style house with two tiny gardens, that the couple brought up four children, all of whom went to grammar school and became in turn a teacher, a ship's captain, a deputy headmistress and a professor. It was their youngest daughter, Kathy, who was to become the academic and, incidentally, my wife.

We both read English at Leeds University and I first became aware of her when she had a singing role in – this being 1968 – an anarchist musical put on by the drama group starring a certain Alan Yentob, who was later to become the BBC's Arts Supremo. Her lyrics were accompanied by a discordant melody, which was considerably enhanced by the fact that my wife-to-be had a terrible singing voice. But it was a case of *coup de foudré* and I fell in love that night.

We married four years later and Kathy subsequently accompanied me to America where I became New York correspondent of the *Daily Express* when it sold well over three million copies a day, before joining the then much smaller circulation *Daily Mail* as American Bureau Chief.

Years passed and by now we were back in England where I was climbing – and occasionally stumbling down – the greasy executive ladder on the *Mail*. Rose, by now widowed, was still living in that hugely aspirational home, but all was not well. About a mile away in open countryside, the council had razed woodland, filled in ponds and built four tower blocks, which brutally protruded from this bleak wasteland like accusing fingers. They were built for families from the notoriously impoverished Liverpool 8 area, which was being demolished. The new residents moved in, their old communities decimated and no new community to be found in their sterile homes in the sky.

Indeed, nothing had been done by those architectural geniuses in the planning department to provide any sense of community or to even lay on buses to the shuttered fortresses that passed for local shops. Not surprisingly, the ex-Liverpool 8 children ran riot and soon that established estate of small Georgian-style houses was infested by crime. It was when her house had been burgled seven times and she discovered a youth trying to break in through her toilet window that Kathy and I decided to ask Rose to come to live with us in London.

For the next twenty years, she was a constant feature in our household. She helped teach both my sons to read, and helped in the kitchen when my wife came home exhausted. Possessed of almost surreal serenity, she radiated a warm, calming influence throughout our home – especially when my eldest son, by then twelve, was off school for a year with illness. I don't think I have ever seen a prouder woman than Rose when, a year later, he won a scholarship to Eton.

Five years ago, at the age of ninety, she was diagnosed with stomach cancer. In hospital she was, against her express wishes, put in a mixed-sex ward, an indignity that – I exaggerate not – traumatised her. Later she was to refuse an operation which might have prolonged her life a little, preferring to spend her last days in our home which was, of course, by then *her* home.

She died in her own bed with her family around her, overlooking the garden she loved, stroking Freddie, our Cairn terrier, who had always made her laugh.

The reason I'm telling you all of this is that I believe that the most disturbing aspect of modern British social culture is the way many of our elderly are treated.

Put to one side the scandal of shunting them off to those soulless and often cruel battery farms called old folks' homes. Equally worrying is the way that, too often, we airbrush them from our lives instead of welcoming them into our homes and lives where they can make such a rich contribution to the family unit.

Over the years, I have asked politicians from both the Left and Right of the political spectrum why they don't give tax breaks to those who look after their own parents. It seems lunacy that we do so little to encourage families to look after their own relatives, instead spending more and more taxpayers' money to finance the ever-burgeoning old folks' industry.

My boys learned so much from their grandma. They learned about the dignity of the elderly, their selfless patience, kind generosity and wisdom. They learned about illness and how it is possible to cope with it with quiet resignation. Above all, they learned how a contented death, while immeasurably sad, can have a moving beauty that can actually be life-enhancing for those who remain behind.

That is what Rose taught my family. To have put her in a home would have been *our* loss. For modern 'civilised' Britain to consign so many of its elderly into anonymous homes is *its* loss.

Paul Dacre is Editor of the Daily Mail *and Editor-in-Chief of Associated Newspapers.*

Making Crowdie

Caitlin Davies

When I stayed the night with Grandma Marion this is what she did before we went to bed: she took an old pair of beige tights, as thin and sticky as spiders' webs, and into the tights she poured some rotten milk. The kitchen windows of her Carlisle bungalow were hazy with condensation from the tatties she'd made earlier, boiled for my tea until they were soft as clouds. But Grandma Marion didn't come from Carlisle; she came from the Highlands of Scotland, and tonight she was making crowdie.

When the tights were full, she tied a knot at the end and then she hung them, soft and saggy, from the kitchen ceiling. I don't remember how, but the toes of the tights just grazed the sink. 'Waste not want not,' said Grandma Marion, pleased to have found good use both for the milk and the tights.

In the morning she had her bath in a carefully measured one inch of water and dried her hair that was a pale blue, the result of a botched rinse job that she hadn't seemed to have noticed. Then she took down the tights that had hung from the kitchen ceiling all night long like bloated legs and with a knife she scraped out the crowdie. I thought the cream cheese would taste of tights, but it was creamy and crumbly and only slightly sour.

'"O that I had ne'er been married,"' said Grandma Marion reciting Robbie Burns, '"I wad never had nar care, Now I've gotten wife an' weans, An' they cry 'Crowdie' evermair."'

Then she made the morning's porridge, using oats that had also been soaked overnight, and stirring only clockwise in the pan so the Devil wouldn't get the cook. She put my porridge in a white bowl and placed it in the front room on a fold-out tray, its metal legs opening like a concertina, the surface printed with faded red flowers. Around my mound of porridge was a moat of milk. Then I ate the porridge with salt. Grandma Marion kept sugar in her sideboard, lots and lots of fat white packets of sugar because there could be another war, but I wasn't allowed that.

She ate her own porridge in the kitchen, standing up. I could see her through the serving hatch, bowl in hand, staring out on to her winter back garden. I don't know why she stood up; it seemed to show respect for the porridge. But then Grandma Marion did everything standing up; for an hour or more she could stand by the stove reading *Oliver Twist*. With the porridge we had tea, the pot kept warm under a tartan cosy, and then

Grandma Marion read my tealeaves. She swirled my empty cup and turned it this way and that until, to her apparent surprise, there was usually a letter to be seen, as well as a tall dark stranger.

After breakfast I was allowed to lick all the Green Shield stamps she'd saved and stick them, carefully, one by one, in the little book until it became too bumpy to close. She stood, waiting until I was done, two damp green slices of cucumber on her eyes, left over from an unfinished sandwich. 'Waste not want not,' said Grandma Marion.

But she had an even better trick for tired eyes. When she made scrambled eggs, after she'd broken an egg into a bowl, then she'd scrape out the thin mucusy coating on the inside of the eggshell.

'What's on your face, Grandma?' I asked the first time I saw her do this.

'Oh!' she said, delighted, fluttering her eyelashes. 'Can you see the difference?'

'Yes, Grandma,' I told her, staring in wonder at the mosaic of eggshell stuck on her eyelids and waiting for her to say, 'Waste not…'

Caitlin Davies is a freelance journalist and the author of Jamestown Blues, The Return of El Negro, Place of Reeds *and* Black Mulberries. *Her latest novel,* Friends Like Us, *is out now.*

A Transatlantic Tale
Hilton Dawson

A grandparent now myself I have good thoughts and some memory of all four of my own.

While I enjoyed long relationships with both my grandmothers it is sad that both my grandfathers died when I was a young child and important to reflect that the four of them could each have written their own stories. They were all worthy of a bigger mark on the world.

Perhaps it was because they lived so close to us in a small village and were so part of my early routine, so present in my early years that I hardly thought of them having a life before or beyond my regular visits for tea. Bashful and oversensitive as a child it's possible that I wasn't sure that I should ask.

It took a visit to an isolated house thousands of miles away in rural Maine, myself much older and all my grandparents long dead, before they all became more real.

My maternal granddad's letters did it. Shown to me by my half-cousin Charlie they'd been sent by Tom Renner, then a Northumbrian pitman with a wife and family of his own, to Maud – the sister whom he never would or could expect to see again. Almost a century ago she had emigrated to America in service to a wealthy family and had then travelled the continent to California and back to the far north-east, almost to Canada.

Carefully preserved after crossing the Atlantic and traversing the whole United States the letters made clear the strong bonds between a brother and sister who had lost both parents as children in the hard years of the early twentieth century. They described the ordinary life of a young man, his wife and baby daughter far removed from the rather frail old people that I had known and they expressed feelings that might have been less easily conveyed in person. For those of us who now know the way the story turned out there is a dreadful poignancy in every word.

Tragically Maud died in the winter of 1929 after giving birth to Charlie in a lonely wood cabin in the hamlet of Grindstone, Maine. Now nothing more than a lorry park near the logging roads it's a place that must have seemed as hard and cold and unforgiving as its name. Answered just before she died, bringing warmth to a frightening isolation I could well believe that at such a time these letters from home may have been the most precious scraps of paper in the world.

However, I still wondered how they had survived through all the tragedy and upset of a young woman dying just at the moment when her son required so much work and all the attention of the newly born.

Then, driving away, I recalled my granny, by then Tom's widow, telling me of the 'old lady' – Charlie's paternal grandmother – who had taken him into her care and sent regular letters to the relatives she would never meet detailing his progress over the years. The letters were wrapped in good quality hand-me-downs which helped the English family through the tough years of the thirties and the tales of Charlie as a boy were enclosed within more general news of Mr Roosevelt and the New Deal.

The 'old lady' had obviously been as careful to preserve all the relics of his mother for her grandson as she was meticulous in keeping contact with his relatives so far away.

Pre-dating Alistair Cooke, my granny's letters from America set out the tide of social history in a country far away and left her with an indelible impression that the New Deal was a good thing. From a Northumbrian fishing village where our family had lived for uncounted generations, she also helped to explain to a family who had long lived off the bountiful land of America why the half-English grandson might just have a passion – eventually requited over a lifelong career – for the sea.

I flew back from holiday in a few hours and dropped Charlie an email to tell him we were home, reflecting on the changes since my grandparents lived their lives.

I remain utterly moved that one of the later possessions kept carefully in that far distant house for so many years was a photo of another cherished first grandson, a young English child – of me.

POSTSCRIPT

Showing this piece to my mother, now aged eighty-four, she reminded me that one of Maud's last acts was to write out cards with the announcement and details of Charlie's birth. They arrived in Northumberland in the same envelope as the letter telling my grandparents that she had died. Carefully handed down to my mam she keeps them safe and wonders whether it's now time to send them home to Charlie and to Maud's grandchildren and great-grandchildren.

Hilton Dawson is the Chair of the National Academy for Parenting Practitioners.

My Perfect Grandparents

Isla Dewar

I have often lamented my lack of grandparents. They all died before I was old enough to get to know them. I have only a glimmer of a memory of one of them, my father's mother who lived in Edinburgh's Stockbridge.

I remember her shoes (well, I was only two and they were the part of her closest to my face). The shoes were black, highly polished, low-heeled and laced up past her ankles. They were comfortably shaped by years of wear, her feet would have been happy in them. I remember her stockings, grey, wrinkled at the knees. Her dress, patterned with blue and grey flowers. Her face, however, is a blur. I can never conjure it up.

I know I missed a lot. At school friends would talk about their grans and grandpas. They'd show off presents they'd been given, boast about trips they'd been taken on or just chat about the comfortable older couple who always had time for them.

Not wanting to miss out on such conversations, I invented two sets of fabulous grandparents. One couple had been killed in the war fighting for the French Resistance. The other was rarely around – they worked for a travelling circus. My imaginary grandfather had retired from a daring life as a trapeze artist, whirling through the air in a spangled outfit and was now helping out with the lion taming. My imaginary grandmother was a bareback rider. I was a childhood liar. Actually my grandfather had been a hairdresser, his wife a seamstress. But I like to think they would have enjoyed the fantasy.

I also forgive myself for envying my husband who had the best, most supportive and liveliest grandparents of anyone I know. His father's mother lived till she was in her nineties, ate a great deal of porridge, and, dressed in a long black coat, walked for miles and miles every day. She walked for the simple pleasure of walking. She made a living as a bookie's runner. This wasn't exactly legal, but it helped with the bills. Her family visited every Sunday. They'd gather round the fire and discuss local gossip and the price of coal, before dining on steak pie and mashed potatoes. She offered her grandchildren an ever-open door. She had time for them. She had patience; she listened. She was the one they ran to when things went wrong. She was loved.

When I grow up – something I'm working on – I know the kind of granny I want to be. Flamboyant, independent and a little bit reckless, doing all the things I didn't have the nerve to do when I was younger. I'll be the granny in purple.

It's odd when you think about it, that the stereotypical grandmother should be depicted as an old woman with a cauliflower perm, grey cardigan and wide-fitting slippers. I know many grandmothers, and none of them look like that. Mostly they like to imagine they're as sassy as Helen Mirren, sing like Aretha Franklin, dance like Tina Turner – though they glumly accept their miniskirt days are over and most complain that their knees are older than they are.

They all work. They have busy social lives. Yet, they are qualified to be grannies – they can make soup, they can do sums in their heads, they understand apostrophes, they have patience with little people, and they all know when to keep their mouths shut.

But they all agree that holding their first grandchild was one of the most moving and fulfilling moments of their lives. They speak of the joy of having little people in their lives again. And of that other joy when those same little people are dispatched home after an exhausting afternoon. They have all the pleasure of children without the hard work and the guilt of parenthood.

They also have the wisdom of time and experience. They know that children don't last as long as they'd like them to. Children grow up. The inevitable happens, they

leave home. So grandparents know that these small boisterous people in their lives are a passing pleasure and are
aware that they should enjoy them while they can.

My husband's maternal grandfather spent a lot of
time with him, and the man had a huge and lasting influence on him. He was a political campaigner and went
round the villages in north-east Scotland, giving rousing
speeches. He could silence rowdy rooms with a single
imperious peer over the top of his spectacles.

Knowing he might not be around to see his grandchild educated, he read the classics to him before he
learned to read. Realising he was getting a little too old
and stiff to keep up with a wilful, headstrong child, he
trained his sheepdog to round him up and herd him
home when he strayed. I have no idea what current
authorities would make of that today. But it worked. And
my husband has a normal man/dog relationship with
our golden retriever.

The thing my husband remembers most about his
grandfather is his hand. It reached down to take his
when they went out for walks together.

One of the greatest pleasures of children, and one
that I miss now both of mine are grown up, is the small
warm hand in yours. Taking a child's hand is such a
simple act of trust and affection, you can almost neglect
its importance. It is a gentle intimacy that makes walking
side by side precious.

One day, when I'm a granny in purple expounding about the sixties, introducing my children's children to Bob Dylan, Leonard Cohen and The Stones, I shall take a little hand in mine and walk. Walking with children is such bliss. They have many original thoughts to offer. The world is still new to them; they are not daunted by it. I remember asking my son if he knew the meaning of life. He was four at the time. I wasn't expecting a profound reply, I just wondered what he thought. He told me the meaning of life was not crying when you lost at dominoes. That'll do for me. The more I think about it, the more I realise it's better than anything I could have come up with.

I would like to think that I could take my grandchild's hand and lead them into the future. But, I know now that wouldn't be the case. Children have a very strong sense of the present, and the future is theirs. They'll be leading me.

Isla Dewar lives in Fife with her husband – a cartoonist and illustrator – and a golden retriever. She has written ten novels and a couple of books for reluctant readers. She has two sons neither of whom has yet produced a grandchild.

Lorna Edwards

In life, I have had so many labels, from being a daughter, a teacher, a wife, a mother and recently a pensioner. Each time I change my role, I pine for the one that has gone. There I was, planning my retirement, when my eldest daughter announced that she was pregnant. Since the birth of my first grandson, I have earned a new title of 'Grandma'. This new role has changed my life and my relationship with my daughter. I feel needed again and it's a great feeling. A year later my youngest daughter joined the group when her own daughter was born. What more could I ask for?

Then the website grannynet.co.uk was conceived. It is the brainchild of my youngest daughter who has set up a support website for grandparents. My involvement is mainly talking things through and floating ideas about where to go next. Since its launch in February 2008, I have been interviewed by the national papers, talked to a wide variety of grandparents at the Olympia Retirement show, while discovering that I am able to empathise with a wide range of people and that my daughter and I make a great team. There is a need out there for us grandparents to have a voice and this website has given us the tool. Since then we have been on the BBC World Service to talk to other grandparents around the world. The gentle voice of Eveline talking about her life in South Africa now that whole generations of parents have been wiped our by Aids will haunt me for a long time.

I feel so privileged to be part of the new group of grandparents who still have so much to give, and have begun to embrace the technological world of search engines and forums in order to support, love and understand their children and grandchildren. Long may we continue to adapt and learn. I love my new role as a grandparent and advisor to the website. I can't wait to see what next year will bring.

Lorna Edwards is co-founder of Grannynet.co.uk

Richard Eyre

I have no fond memories of grandparents. Both my mother's parents died before I was born. My paternal grandmother, according to my father's somewhat partial view, had been worn out by long periods of silent disdain from her husband followed by eruptions of volcanic bullying.

My grandfather lived in an isolated late-eighteenth-century house in a small village in North Devon. The house stood in a few acres of parkland dominated by a huge horse-chestnut tree. On the front of the house two of its large windows were blocked up, which gave the face of the house the look of blindness, as if its eyelids had been sewn together. My grandfather was not rich. He came from a military family and had seen little of his father, who had died when he was eight, having given up most of his adult life to defending the perimeters of the British Empire. My grandfather followed his father into the army but he had a desultory career and retired early, having reached the rank of major. I asked my father once what his father had done during his war, The Great War. 'Sat twenty miles behind the lines at HQ warming his arse on a stove,' he said.

He lived on his major's pension and the evidence for this was all too obvious in what he would never have called his lifestyle. If the past is another country, it's one in which he'd settled long ago. He'd stopped his personal clock somewhere before the First World War and he always dressed as an Edwardian: narrow-trousered pale brown tweed suits and a high-necked round-edged stiff collar, or breeches with puttees and a Norfolk jacket. He was not amused to be told, shortly before he died in the 1950s, that he was a real Teddy boy, even if his hair, shaved Prussian-style close to his scalp, rather spoiled the joke. If he had a role model it must have been Bismarck, although the suggestion that he resembled a German would have earned the retort: 'I hate the bloody Germans. And the bloody French. And the bloody Italians, for that matter.'

His house was warmed, and I use the word advisedly, by one fire in the dining room and another in his bedroom. There was a firm and unbreakable rule about the fires: they were never to be lit before the first of October or after the first of April. If it snowed on the second of April, so be it; you complained at your peril. He never had electricity or central heating installed in the house. All the lighting came from candles and oil-lamps, all cooking was on a large black open coal-burning range in a kitchen with a flagstoned floor and a smoke-stained ceiling. The water was pumped in the yard where there was a well, inhabited by dead cats, rats and frogs. I wish I exaggerated. The sole concession to the twentieth century was a large radio, powered by an accumulator. Its use was permitted only twice a day: the *Nine O'Clock News* in the morning and the *Nine O'Clock News* at night.

To a child's eye the house offered a continent of fearful possibilities: dark panelled labyrinthine corridors, cellars, creaking floorboards, cupboards that were never opened, rooms that were never entered. The drawing room was forbidden territory. It was the only room in the house that was light in colour and airy and cheerful in feeling. We never used it. The grand piano that had been played by my grandmother remained locked and her collection of musical boxes lay untouched. Her spirit was a presence in the room, and to creep into the room unobserved was to find a calm sanctuary from the potential terrors that lay in the rest of the house.

There were two lavatories, one set at the end of a stone-floored tack room, unheated and supplied only with old shredded copies of *The Times* for use as lavatory paper, the other more comfortable but reserved exclusively for the use of women. Women were not, however, allowed to enter my grandfather's smoking room, whose purpose seemed to be as much to exclude women as to smoke a pipe. Its walls were spread with haphazardly hung rows of sporting and military prints, sepia photographs of army officers and brown-paper-covered dog-eared copies of the Army List dating from the 1880s. It smelt musty and, on the rare occasions that I was allowed in, seemed as welcoming as a monk's cell.

My sister and I were set household tasks: pumping the water in the yard, cleaning the funnels of the oil lamps, rubbing the rust off the old iron cutlery, and sometimes, as a treat offered by my grandfather to provoke my father, fetching rough cider from the barrel in the cellar in a heavy thick glass jug. At the age of six or seven, we would be encouraged to drink this potent local brew and it never failed to provoke a heady vagueness in us and a full-scale row between them.

The rows were always staged in the dining room – a long, high, dingy room with plum-coloured wallpaper, dominated by a portrait of a stern patriarch with a large walrus moustache in full military regalia: my great-grandfather. His son always sat beneath the portrait and stared malevolently at my father, who sat at the opposite end of the thick oak table. My grandfather cast a sepulchral silence over meals, punctuated occasionally by a timid dribble of conversation from my sister or from me. She told me once that she'd met someone on a train and talked to him. My grandfather slammed his fist on the table, shaking the glasses and the cutlery: 'No one's ever spoken to me in a train, thank Christ!'

It was the rows that first alerted me to the possibilities of drama. I was fascinated not so much by the obvious entertainment of inventive streams of violent invective as much as the silences that followed: epic, giant, immense, terrible and terrifying. Maybe they're magnified by the eyes of childhood but to me each look had the weight of a hammer blow, each blink a fist. Only the scraping of the cutlery on the plates distracted from the dense absence of words and broke the thickness of the space between them. It was as if the atoms in the air were charged with the anger that they generated. When my mother spoke the storm would break again, thunderous threats culminating in my mother leaving the room in tears, my sister and I silent as sea anemones and the two men standing with their fists extended at each other while the shadows made by the flickering oil lamps danced on the dark ceiling.

Outside his family my grandfather's displays of violence were rare but celebrated. Several times he was bound over to keep the peace for assaulting motorists with a horsewhip. He saw himself as a private avenger, keeping the roads free of the alien motor car. When he heard, or more likely scented, an approaching car he would position his horse across a narrow lane, forcing the driver to stop and plead to be allowed to pass. Iron-hearted, confirmed in his role as the Scourge of Progress, he resisted all pleas for mercy. The driver would be wound to a pitch of exasperation and get out of his car to move the stubborn object. Then he would be lashed for his insolence and my grandfather would ride on. 'That'll teach you, you bastard!'

He was even-handed in his brutality and dealt with his son in the same currency. My father was taught to ride before he could walk, tied to a saddle before his legs reached the stirrups. The consequence was that he trusted animals more than people and, try as he might, he could never quite find fellow feeling with those who had less rigorous childhoods than his own. When my father died his cousin wrote to me, saying that while he knew that I'd had a difficult relationship with my father, I must understand that it was a wonder that my father had survived his childhood at all. He told me that he had once – and only once – visited my grandfather to introduce him to his fiancée. After molesting the fiancée in the gooseberry patch, my grandfather had showed the cousin round the house. In his bedroom, there was a sort of animal skin on the floor. He stared at it, slightly misty-eyed. 'Viceroy,' he said, 'Best damn pony I ever had.'

Richard Eyre is a theatre, film and opera director. He was Director of the National Theatre from 1987 to 1997. His last film was Notes on a Scandal *and he has just directed* The Last Cigarette *at the National Theatre and* The Last Cigarette *in the West End.*

Some Grandparenting Tips
Jane Fearnley-Whittingstall

Today's grandparents are very different from the stereotypical granny with grey bun and cardigan and the stooping granddad with walking stick and hairy tweed jacket. But some things haven't changed. We still get untold joy from time spent with our grandchildren, and although many grandparents are still working and have busy social lives, we willingly give our grandchildren priority when planning our lives. Spending time with them is not a chore. It's one of life's greatest pleasures.

Many modern families with both parents working full-time could not function without the help of grandparents, and, when a request for childminding comes along, many are happy to drop everything, even at short notice. But we shouldn't always feel obliged to do so – the relationship works best when our children understand that we also have lives of our own to lead. One mum explained, 'My mother-in-law sometimes refuses, so when she agrees I know it's all right and I'm not imposing on her.'

To help the relationship between grandparents and parents go as smoothly as that between grandparents and grandchildren, here are a few tips, gathered from mothers as well as grandmothers:

- *Know when to zip your lip*

  Tact is a highly desirable quality in a grandparent. Try not to give advice unless you are asked for it, and even then, tread warily. Young parents are sensitive to any hint of criticism of their methods of childcare, and however much we may disapprove of a toddler being offered a choice at mealtimes, as if in a restaurant, or a four-year-old sleeping in his parents' bed every night, we will, if we are wise, keep quiet about it.

- *Never, ever say…*

  A maddened mum begged me to pass on this message: 'please please please don't tell us that we were all dry through the night by eighteen months. No matter how many times I hear this *I don't believe you*!'

- *Go equipped*

  When looking after babies or toddlers, wear clothes with large pockets and fill them with tissues. You'll need them to wipe noses (there is virtually no closed season for runny noses), chocolatey mouths, sticky fingers and grazed knees. Keep in your handbag, your car and your house a supply of treats to hand out as rewards, bribes and comforters. If sweets are taboo, make do with raisins or organic fruity snack bars.

- *Make your house safe*
  Don't be the granny whose grandchild locked himself in the lavatory, fell out of the window or drank the washing-up liquid. Check your house for safety before grandchildren visit, putting ornaments and pot plants out of reach (out of the extended reach, that is, of a child standing on a chair). If floor-level cupboards don't have locks, or you have lost the key, tie the handles together or seal temporarily with masking tape.

- *Make yourself popular with the parents*
  The one thing parents of little ones long for above everything is a lie-in in the morning. To make sure they get it, invite the grandchildren into your bed for a morning cuddle and story, give them breakfast and get them dressed.

- *Make yourself popular with the children*
  Keep a few toys and books at your house for each age group, preferably different from those they have at

home, so that 'Granny's toys' and books seem special. They don't have to be new and expensive – charity shops and car boot sales are good sources – and you can have fun seeking out vintage favourites from your own childhood.

● *Practice makes perfect*

We grandparents all admit to having trouble folding and unfolding the buggy or pushchair. Don't get caught in the supermarket car park struggling with a bundle of tangled metal, while the baby screams blue murder in the car and the toddler disappears over the horizon. Practise, practise and practise till you have mastered the art.

● *Acquire the knowledge*

Learn the difference between Tinky-winky, Dipsy, Lala and Po. They are today's equivalent of Flopsy, Mopsy, Cottontail and Peter, or Florence, Zebedee, Dougal and Brian. And be reassured that Thomas, Edward, Henry and Percy still occupy adjacent engine sheds under the watchful eye of the Fat Controller, and are as popular as ever.

● *Keep in touch*

If you don't see your grandchildren regularly, keep in touch by telephone, email or texting and they are less likely to be shy when you meet. Even babies, who can only gurgle in reply, like the sound of a familiar voice on the phone. Older children also love getting post-cards and occasional little presents through the post.

- *Be the family historian*
  Do tell your grandchildren all you know about family history, and what life was like when you were young. It may make them yawn now, but if you don't tell them about the characters in the family album, when they are older they'll wish they'd asked you while you were still there to satisfy their curiosity.

- *Your second childhood*
  All too soon they will grow up, so, from the wonderful moment when you first make your grand-children's acquaintance, enjoy their company. Indulge in an unashamed second childhood by join-ing in their games, whether it involves crawling around on the floor being a dinosaur or putting on a tinsel crown to play the part of a princess.

Jane Fearnley-Whittingstall is a writer and garden designer. Her books include the Good Granny *series.*

Sir Alex Ferguson

Football has always been an interruption in the Ferguson Family: my three sons were all born on the day I had a game. Likewise our first grandson arrived the night before we won the League at Ipswich. As we sat around the dinner table that evening my thoughts were more on how my daughter-in-law Tania was coping, and what was keeping her in delivering our first grandchild! Jason phoned us with regular updates but it still felt like a long wait.

When the call finally came to tell me that Jake Alexander Ferguson was born a healthy young lad, the only thing I had to do was open the champagne. The next day I heard the news that the great racing driver Ayrton Senna had been killed in a race. I reflected how one day may welcome a new child into the world and the very next day see a great hero depart it.

On the Monday I took my family down to London to see our boy at Queen Charlotte Hospital, Chiswick. Of course, granny had been staying with Jason and Tania before the birth – nothing official happens without her first being present.

Jake is now fourteen and a credit to his parents, but he has to share the attention with his twin sisters Sophie and Ella, younger brother Harvey, and Ruby, who is now four and bosses everyone about. When I tease her she tells me to buzz off, which is nice of her.

The Ferguson clan has grown at a very fast pace lately and we now total ten grandchildren. On most weekends we have usually about three or four with us and this is where the difference lies between your own children, and having grandchildren. Nowadays I can't get on my computer, the snooker table is always occupied, the telly is on children's programmes, the fridge is raided, not a biscuit in sight. My oldest son Mark lives in London and his first-born, Hamish, gives me tactical advice on my team: who should be playing and all the mistakes of each game are embedded in his mind – oh, and by the way, he's only six! He said to me after one game 'If Nani had a better first touch he would have scored yesterday,' so who am I to argue with experts.

I enjoy watching their progress because when my sons were growing up I missed a lot of that simply because I was hardly ever in the house. I was running two public houses in Glasgow and managing St Mirren Football Club so Cathy looked after everything. She always said when the boys got older they would migrate towards me and it was partly true, because by that time I was managing Aberdeen full-time and found I had more time for the family.

When I was young I had the good fortune to know my great-grandfather Beaton and my great-grandmother Mansell. I have a black-and-white photograph of the four generations on my father's side at home, my great-grandfather, my grandmother, my father and myself. In fact, all my cousins and I were born in the back bedroom at my granny's house. They later immigrated to Canada in the fifties and still live there.

My grandmother on my mother's side, granny Irwin, was a star. She played a big part in bringing up me and my brother because both my parents worked. Her mother's house was a gathering place for granny Irwin's six siblings and their offspring. Every one of us remembers great-granny Mansell's little old house so well, with its gas mantle above the fireplace and her rocking chair. I still recall her once smoking some kind of pipe. She was a tough old bird and everyone obeyed whatever she said. Yes, including me.

I had the unusual fortune to have four grandparents when growing up, unlike my own grandchildren who have not had the pleasure. But you can't have everything – although try telling them that!

Alex Ferguson CBE is a former football player and the Manager of Manchester United Football Club.

Emma Freud

If it's all right, I'd like to write a word or two about my dear dad and his grandfather. My father grew up in the strange shadow of a grandfather who was the founder of psychoanalysis. He probably had two choices – to be very proud of Sigmund Freud or to pretend he didn't exist. My dad went for the latter – so he never read a word Freud wrote, never owned a book by him and never discussed him except *as* a grandfather, a job that apparently Sigmund did quite well.

My father was once on the Johnny Carson chat show in America and Carson – going against the strict instructions of 'whatever you ask, don't mention Sigmund' – said 'Tell me about your grandfather?' My dad gave a long and detailed account of his maternal grandfather and his work as a German banker. Carson moved on.

The one time my father might have been able to exploit Sigmund turned out rather badly. He was on a parliamentary delegation to Japan when he was an MP. The hotel they stayed in had only one top room and my father, who was the senior politician in the group, was rather put out when the only suite was given to Winston

Churchill, MP, instead of him. He asked the receptionist why, and was told it was because Mr Churchill had a famous grandfather. For the first time in his life he had been out-grandfathered.

As a result of my father's unusual position on all this, my siblings and I never read a line of the great man's writings or knew anything about him. I think my sister had it worst. At the age of seven she came home from school one day and said, 'Who is Sigmund Freud? The teachers were talking about him as though I should know.' My father told her that Sigmund was her grandfather, and was indeed quite well known. He quietly explained that he hadn't mentioned him to her before now because it was slightly embarrassing, as Sigmund Freud had invented the flush toilet. After that, my sister changed the subject instantly whenever anyone mentioned her unfortunate ancestor.

Once my father became a grandfather himself, he continued the theme of playing down professional achievements. He had no interest in my four children reading his books, listening to him on the radio or regaling them with stories of his life as a journalist and politician – but he did well with jokes and backgammon and cookery tips.

As a fabulously eccentric cook, I think his most important legacy to them may well have been his recipe for 'Drunkard's Soup'. You soften a chopped onion in a lot of butter till near caramelised. Add a bottle of champagne. When the champagne is hot, float a small camembert on top till it has melted.

The champagney-buttery-oniony liquor with a hunk of melted cheese at its centre is about as good an inheritance as any grandfather could have handed down. And probably more useful to them in the end than *Introductory Lectures on Psychoanalysis* could ever have been to me.

Emma Freud has been a broadcaster on radio and TV since 1985. For the last twenty years she has worked for Comic Relief and is now Director of Red Nose Day as well as a patron of the White Ribbon Alliance. She also works as script editor or associate producer to her partner Richard Curtis on all his film and TV work.

Michael Fuller

I met Stanley Theaphelous Fuller, my paternal grandfather, for the first time when I was twenty-six years old. My parents came to the UK from Jamaica in the 1950s and I was born in London in 1959. I visited Jamaica for the first time in 1985. My parents grew up in Portland, which is on the north-east coast of Jamaica. Being a great fan of James Bond, I am proud that Ian Fleming made Jamaica his home. In 1985 the area was undeveloped and I recall taking a very bumpy car ride along dirt roads to meet my grandfather.

I have a vivid memory of walking up a grassy track to my grandfather's house, a small wooden shack nestling between banana trees. Stanley Fuller welcomed me with a warm smile and a wave of his hand from where he sat on his front porch. We talked for hours and explored the family land packed with banana trees. I visited the places where my parents had grown up with names such as Fairy Hill and Happy Grove.

Stanley Fuller was born on 23 March 1905 and lived his whole life in Portland. He was the village tailor and made suits for anyone who could afford to buy one. He was also a farmer who grew bananas and other produce. Stanley was married to Icilda Beckford, with whom he produced nine children, including my father. He taught his older children how to hem the lining of a jacket and paid them two shillings and sixpence at the end of each week. They would use the money to treat the younger ones with candy and ice cream. Stanley was strong willed and was known for his sharp memory. He had one remedy for all ailments: Vick's vapour rub.

For much of his life Stanley believed that he should keep his money close by, so he would put it in a paper bag and hide it in the ceiling. One morning he noticed lots of little pieces of paper on the floor below the ceiling where he kept his money. To his horror, rats had found his paper bag. From then on he would make regular trips to the bank.

My grandfather died on 9 May 2007, at the great age of one hundred and two, in a comfortable home that his daughter, my aunt Joyce, had built for him years earlier to replace the old shack. My aunt, a qualified nurse, had cared for my grandfather in his later years. He credited his long life to his daily portion of aloe vera and a glass of 'Portland Bush', a foul-tasting homemade brew with the colour of brown dirty water. After tasting this vile concoction I realised that my prospects of reaching the same great age as my grandfather were limited by the reluctance of my taste buds to experience it again.

A few years ago my father returned to live in Jamaica. Like so many of his generation who came to the UK from the Caribbean in the 1950s, he has built himself a house and 'gone home'. I can see the attraction of retiring to a familiar place with a slower pace of life and better weather. But I feel sadness for the grandchildren who are growing up with their grandparents so far away, as I did myself. My visit to Portland and meeting my grandfather was a life-changing experience that I will never forget.

Michael Fuller is currently the Chief Constable of Kent Police. He is Britain's first black Chief Constable, taking up this role in January 2004. He is also a non-practicing barrister and won the Queen's Police Medal for distinguished service in July 2004.

Katherine Grainger

I consider myself very lucky when it comes to grandparents. I knew all four of mine from my earliest days until I was a grown adult and, as a result, have endless precious memories of them, especially the two who lived in Aberdeen.

My sister Sarah and I spent most summer holidays with Gran and Grandad and we were spoilt rotten. Anything was possible when with them. I have lost count of the number of times Sarah and I jumped into the car after pleading to be taken to Aberdeen beach whatever the weather! The four of us sat, often alone on the beach, behind the multicoloured windbreak as the wind battered us, eating sandwiches which slowly filled with sand before rushing down into the freezing North Sea to paddle. Sarah and I were absolutely in our element while Gran and Grandad looked on dutifully, wrapping us in towels when we came out of the sea, taking photos, making sure we were safe and happy and feeding us '99' ice creams from the shop on the promenade.

As we grew older we started going to the fairground at the beach as well as playing in the sea. I remember my poor grandad literally turning green on the waltzers as he kept us company and looked after us as we spun endlessly around and around. My grandad was a policeman all his life and protected and cared for us every second we were with him.

My gran was born to be a gran. It was as if she stepped into the world ready for that job. She was one of those amazing natural cooks who always had flour-dusted recipe books but as far as I can remember never even so much as glanced at them as she effortlessly moved around the kitchen picking up ingredients, adding a handful here, a pinch there, a dash of something (sometimes alcoholic) and then an hour or so later the most incredible smells would filter out of the kitchen. Nobody went hungry if my gran was in the house, whether they were friends, family, strangers or pets. Or prisoners – but that's another story! There was always a constant supply of delicious homemade goodies being pressed into your hands. One day I hope those genes will be evident in my skills in the kitchen, but I'm still waiting.

My gran could also make anything from nothing. We have great photos of Sarah and I carrying little plastic golf clubs around the garden in tartan golf bags. Golf bags made by my gran in literally not much more than half an hour after our request. No warning; no pattern: yet perfect. Everything had been thought of in their construction. They were of tartan material with the main section for the clubs, pockets for the golf balls, little elastic straps for the golf tees and shoulder straps for us to carry them around. I think somewhere Julie Andrews is kicking herself now that she didn't think of that for the Von Trapp kids.

My gran could also talk for Britain and was forever filling you in on the details of everyone's life in the neighbourhood and beyond. She was a dynamic, vibrant person and loved life. She loved knowing and learning things and was so proud of us as kids that I have no doubt the poor neighbours had to listen to stories of all of our achievements over and over again. I remember her telling one friend about my sister graduating from university with a first. My sister corrected her saying she hadn't got a first but my gran waved away that slight inaccuracy as a minor detail. She deeply believed Sarah and I were capable of anything, so if we didn't actually achieve everything that was okay, because we were still capable of it and were the best in the world to her; nothing could diminish that view of us.

Looking back now I can fully appreciate that sense of complete and unconditional love, belief and devotion given to us by both Gran and Grandad. It helped us to do things to make them even more proud, but of course they couldn't have been any more proud of us than they already were. Our accomplishments pleased them more because they knew things like that made us happy and in the end that's what they wanted for us – to be happy.

I remember a few years ago after Mum had been talking for hours on the phone with Gran, she came off the phone and commented how much Gran could talk, saying, 'If I ever get like that you must tell me.' Well, my mum is like my gran already in many wonderful ways and I can only hope that those similarities continue, because to have another person like Gran in the family is great with me. Although Mum may have to brush up on her golf-bag making skills…

Katherine Grainger is Britain's most successful female rower with three Olympic silver medals and four world championship gold medals to her name. Alongside rowing she is also studying for a PhD in homicide.

Paul Greengrass

When I was very young, my grandmother took me every Whitsun for a week's holiday in the Lake District. I would pack my own bag and can still remember the journeys as if they were yesterday – by steam train at the very end of the steam era – from the London suburbs through places of astonishing romance like Rugby, Crewe and Lancaster until eventually, late in the day, we would arrive at our Lakeland paradise in the far north-west.

We would stay in a remote farmhouse a few miles from a small village called Bowland Bridge, and each holiday followed a set routine: visits to Windermere, rides on the boats, tea and scones in the High Street, walks around Tarn Hows, picnics on the endless bracken-strewn Fells with the gigantic beauty of Lakeland spread out before my childish open eyes.

And in the evenings we would eat Kendal mint cake and play cards together – Canasta, Whist, Gin Rummy, Beggar My Neighbour – or Scrabble or I-Spy, or tell jokes until my sides hurt with laughter. By the time it was time for bed, I would sink into the coarse lavender sheets and imagine I was a Swallow hunting Amazons across a dark lake under endlessly blue skies.

Those holidays are amongst my happiest memories of childhood.

Many many years later and as I grew up by degrees, I discovered that my grandmother's life had been a hard and tragic one. She lost her true love in the First World War. After she died his bloodstained last letter was found in a locked drawer in her desk. Eventually she married my grandfather, and had a child – my mother – but there were severe complications at the birth and she was unable to add to her family, as she had wanted. Then my grandfather, while still a relatively young man, developed a degenerative disease, which led to dementia. War came, and while visiting her dying husband in the local sanatorium, her house was destroyed by a V1 bomb. She emerged from the war widowed, homeless and penniless.

The post-war years were a slow and arduous struggle back to suburban respectability. Her small semi-detached house – called bizarrely 'Burma' – was eventually rebuilt. She returned to teaching and became a devoted servant of her school and community. Her rebellious, free-spirited daughter – my mother – married a merchant seaman and moved away to begin her own life. Relations between them were never easy but they both persevered. My grandmother was left alone to tend her husband's grave, and her private memories. There must have been a keen sense for this thrifty, hard-working, fun-loving,

God-fearing, well-intentioned woman, that life had not unfolded as she had intended...

But alone with her on our annual holiday I had no sense of her sadness. Was she thinking about the past as I ran without a care across Bowland Bridge towards the Fells beyond? Did her mind dwell on what might have been as we pulled Spilikins from the pile in the middle of the polished table, or played Twist for the last piece of Kendal Mint Cake? I doubt it. I think her grandchildren were a source of simple undiluted pleasure to her, as she was to us. A final piece of completion. Whatever had been or not been for her did not matter in Lakeland.

And that I think is the essential difference between parenthood and grandparenthood. All the stresses and strains of living and growing and becoming are ever present between a child and a parent, even when they both try to hide them. It's the source of the deepest and most elemental of all our loves and connections.

But between a child and a grandparent the past – and the future – is irrelevant. There are only honeyed days to be enjoyed together free of time – bus rides to the station, *Eagle* comics to be bought, steam engines to be inspected, carriages to be chosen, packed lunches to be put up high, with the simple sustaining promise of a long journey to a far-off land of sky and hill and water...

Paul Greengrass is the critically acclaimed director of Bloody Sunday, United 93 *and two* Bourne *films.*

Baroness Greengross

I was very lucky to have four children who in turn produced nine wonderful grandchildren – ranging from a six-foot-two-inch seventeen-year-old to the youngest who has just celebrated her fourth birthday. The younger ones who have passed the Houses of Parliament and been told that this is where I work now believe that I work inside Big Ben and are thus convinced of my importance as a parliamentarian, making sure that Big Ben's hands go round and tell the proper time.

Two other slightly bigger grandchildren visited Parliament recently on school trips. For them, maybe the biggest highlight was when they discovered that the turntable that turns round the post vans in the yard made a perfect roundabout for thirty seven-year-olds. But they saved their real amazement for when they learned that Henry VIII used Westminster Hall as a tennis court and that, during restorations, one of his tennis balls was found lodged in the rafters. Obviously now they have a full understanding of our parliamentary democracy.

For years my husband, Alan, played Santa Claus at our family Christmas parties. Dressed in the full outfit, complete with bushy white beard, he would distribute presents to all the grandchildren and many of their friends. This tradition was a huge success until some of the older ones began to suspect something was not quite right: whenever Santa was in the room, they noticed that Alan was not. We had to find a way of convincing them that far from being Santa, Alan was actually at the party as well. Our solution was for him, after giving out the presents, to disappear and quickly get changed and for me to put on the full gear with extra cushions for the padding. Alan then returned to the room shouting, 'Quickly, quickly, Santa is just leaving for his sleigh.' Leading them to the window they could just get a glimpse of me in my Santa garb waving them goodbye. The illusion was safe – at least for another year or two.

Grandchildren can be very useful when, for instance, the lock on our front door was found to be jammed when we returned from an outing. Ella's five-year-old hand was the only one that could reach into the letter-box and, with the help of a suitably bent coat hanger, raise the latch. Perfect training for a future career!

Praise from a small child is always particularly welcome, even when it comes from a four-year-old in the back of the car who exclaims, in an albeit unintended, patronising voice 'Well done, Sally' when I reversed the car into a particularly large parking space.

I never cease to be amazed at the pure logic kids display. Like the time five-year-old Alexander phoned to tell me his parents were busy packing for a holiday. 'That's wonderful' I replied 'and what are you doing?' After a long puzzled pause he told me 'I'm talking to you'. Or when six-year-old Polly came into the dining room one Christmas Day and I asked her whether all the children were in the playroom. She looked at me with incredulity and said 'No. I'm here.'

Most of all, though, being friends with my grandchildren is the most important thing for me. Taking two of them to Amsterdam, for instance, and discussing the story of Anne Frank or the dangers of drug addiction; sitting on top of a Dartmoor Tor with them and sharing the wonder and excitement of a huge setting sun.

Above all, I cherish my own children's faces and their look of absolute joy and wonder when their own babies arrived. Their real luck is that they still have all those wonderful grandparent years ahead of them.

Baroness Greengross is a crossbench (independent) member of the House of Lords, Commissioner on the Equality & Human Rights Commission and Chief Executive of the International Longevity Centre in the UK.

Lady Edna Healey

I wish I had known all my grandparents, alas I can only recall my maternal grandmother. Now when I stand by my father's family grave in the lovely churchyard in the heart of the Forest of Dean, I see only their names on the tombstones. I do, however, remember the devotion of my aunt, the daughter who commissioned the little statue there. At least I can see them in the faded sepia photographs, rigid and formal in front of an artificial palm tree in the photographer's studio. I should like to have seen my grandfather in his garden and ask about his work as a plate-layer in the local factory. My grandmother could have told me so much about the births of their seven children and my father's upbringing in the house and the school nearby.

I do have the recollections of my elder brother who remembered being carried on my father's shoulders for the five-mile walk down the hill from Coleford to Park End. He and his father were great walkers; some of his friends walked daily into Wales to work. Few owned their own cars, indeed, before windscreen wipers, many kept their cars standing on bricks in the garage during winter.

Some employers ran a company bus. I remember miners outside our house in the early morning, sitting on their heels in what they called the 'miners' squat', waiting for their bus.

I do remember more of my maternal grandmother. Looking back over eighty-five years, I am a little child again sitting on the kitchen table trying to put on my little button boots and the button hook pinching my skin. Kindly, she offers help and, as the family often reminded me, I reply 'I can do it, don't be soft.'

At the end of her life she came to live with us and I was allowed to carry up her morning porridge which she called 'pap'. My mother adored her, 'She was the most *good* woman I ever knew,' she always said. It was my grandmother who sometimes put my sister and me to bed and taught us to kneel on the cold linoleum and recite a comforting if incomprehensible prayer: 'Gentle Jesus, meek and mild, lookupon a little child, pity my simplicity, suffer me to come to thee.' She leaves the memory of a warm presence, and I still hear her affectionate voice singing 'Edna May, bright as day.'

I never knew her husband, my maternal grandfather, a potter, who I suspect, like many potters, drank heavily. Certainly my mother had a very strong hatred of pubs and the smell of strong drink.

The greatest treat in my childhood was an expedition with my grandmother in a horse-drawn brake to the seaside at Barry in Wales. How I regret that I know so little of their lives, so different from ours. Now that I am ninety my memories of the past joined with theirs would cover more than a century of social history.

So often we say 'I wish I had asked them...' It is worthwhile encouraging children to talk to their grandparents. History lessons would come alive and they might better understand themselves.

Lady Edna Healey is the author of six books and presenter of the award-winning documentary Mrs Livingstone, I Presume *and* One More River, *about the life of Mary Slessor. She is married to Denis Healey and has three children and four grandchildren.*

Jenny
Phil Hogan

Through a time tunnel now I see her, in the fading colours of my recall, at her piano. She sits among her family and plays boogie-woogie (far from the piano repertoire, as we knew it, of school hymns and century-old Northern songs). There is ham for tea. I don't want any of it; shy of the angel cake, the swarm of Sunday cousins, this dark house.

Her hands, performing lively callisthenics, are old but strong. Her grey hair is sprung with the frizz of her ancestors, her jaw set unevenly from her Yorkshire side. Her smile challenges. I fear her wet kiss at the end of the afternoon. I was told, with some pride (when she died), that as a young woman she performed at the local fleapit to silent films.

My gentle grandfather – shrunken with age in his cardigan and polished black boots, his eyes unembarrassed in their love for her ('Jenny! Jenny!') – watches with satisfaction from his chair as she plays. He sucks the flame from a match into the bowl of his pipe, knowing everything I don't.

Phil Hogan, the third of four children, grew up in Yorkshire before moving to London in the 1970s. He is a journalist and novelist and has four children of his own.

West-Coast Capital
Tom Hunter

There's an old saying about nothing ever being free and in our household that notion was instilled in us generation after generation. My dad often gets the credit – and rightly so – for my becoming an entrepreneur, but the story is slightly more complicated. You see, my grandmother actually hired my dad into the family grocery business in New Cumnock and gave him his entrepreneurial spurs.

I never met my granddad but my grandmother, who literally ate, breathed and slept the shop (her flat was above it), was a formidable character who cut such an imposing figure that for me as a wee boy made me slightly fearful, but as with every granny she had a heart of gold. For as long as I can remember she ran that shop until dad took over and she meant a great deal to me, in fact I think she was everyone's granny in New Cumnock; she looked out for us all.

We had one ritual with my granny; Saturday pocket money. It was then you earned your money, because, as I've said, nothing comes free. My two sisters and I would skip upstairs to her flat, take up position one after the other on her knee and have to tell her about our week, warts and all. She had a bit of a bark about her, I guess, as most grandparents do, but it was most certainly worse than her bite. She cared for us, lived through us and instilled a deep admiration in me for a woman who could stand her own in what was then most definitely a man's world.

As a nation we reflect too little on just what lessons we can learn from our elders – although through this book, as ever, Sarah is trying to right that wrong.

Tom Hunter is a serial entrepreneur and philanthropist.

Virginia Ironside

I had two wonderful grannies – and even though they're now dead, when I'm with my grandsons, the whole feeling of a loving relationship between grandmother and grandchild comes roaring back. I like having patience – at last – and for love to flow without being veiled by any of the anxiety I experienced when I was a mother.

You have to work at being a good granny. You can't just take a child's love for granted in the way you can when you're a parent, when the child has no choice but to love you. When a grandchild loves you he or she does so for a reason, and that's especially flattering and comforting.

One of the reasons so many children now seem to suffer from anxiety and depression is said to be not only the lack of a father, in some cases, but also the lack of the presence of grandparents, often due to divorce or separation. But they're so important! A grandparent is the European Court of the family structure. Okay, a mother may shout at you, a father may scold you, but a grandparent is always a final court of appeal, who can sometimes treat the problem with more perspective and compassion that those closer to the child.

I don't have any desire to guide my grandsons' interests. All I hope is that they'll *have* interests, and that I'll be able, once I know what they are, to help them enlarge their worlds and to grow up into adults who are as happy and at ease with themselves as anyone can be.

Virginia Ironside is a journalist, agony aunt and author of the bestselling No! I Don't Want to Join a Bookclub. *Her latest book is* The Virginia Monologues, Twenty Reasons Why Being Old is Great. *She has one son, and two grandsons.*

Lisa Jewell

I was spoilt for grandparents, I had five of them.

The one I liked the best died first, when I was ten. He was Grandpa Jack, my paternal grandfather. He had the aquiline nose that both my father and I now sport and thin English hair combed across his pate. He wore tweed sports jackets and smoked a deadly pipe. He was away from his family for six years during the war and never seemed quite to have slotted back into it, an outsider on the periphery of domesticity, a yes-man to his wife, forever compensating for the years she had had to cope on her own. They lived in a beautiful house in the same part of London as us, with a tiered garden that swept downhill to a paddock full of donkeys. He was a lovely man, I wish I'd had time to know him better.

What do I remember most about him?

The day he dropped my sister's new toy on to the dining-room floor and broke it in half, the sadness on his face that his well-intentioned game had ended so unfortunately.

The next one to die was Granddad Albert, my maternal grandfather. I was twenty. He died in Spain where he and his wife had lived for many years. Albert was my Indian granddad: small, dark, compact, partly Indian, partly something non-specifically European, really very handsome. He had a beauty spot by his mouth. It was deserved. Albert was not a cuddly granddad. He was sullen and stroppy. He did not relish family life; he liked to drink with the men. I think, although I do not know for certain, that he missed his life in India, the ayah and the cook and the sprinklers on the lawn.

What do I remember most about him?

The day he slammed his thumb in the door of the car we were all sitting in, how he brushed away our concern, his stubborn refusal to admit that he was hurt.

Next to go was Doreen, my paternal grandmother. I was twenty-three. She died in an old people's home of old age and Alzheimer's. The Alzheimer's ruined her brain but it also softened her sharp edges. No more anti-Semitic rants or complaints about the discomforts of her existence. She accepted my sister's black boyfriend with a sweet smile. She'd been slightly arty in her youth, a toucher-upper for a photographer to the likes of Noël Coward, married late, too busy having fun and being a modern London girl. Everyone said I'd got my creativity from her. Sometimes we were left with her for an after-noon. Home-made flapjacks and cloudy squash in plastic tumblers that smelled of mothballs. We were always happy to see our mum.

What do I remember most about her?

The pinkness in her cheeks after a Gin & It, the care-free use of words like jaunty and jolly and gay, the girlish backward flapper-kick of her leg to express her light-hearted side.

When I was thirty, Ruby died. Ruby was my nana in Spain, my granddad's second wife, the woman who raised my mother. She was delicate, birdlike, half-Portuguese, half-Indian, like her husband. Her hair was soft and her eyes were round and as innocent and expressive as a child's. We stayed with Nana and Granddad when we were tiny, when they lived in Hendon, not in Spain. My mother was in hospital, waiting to have our sister, with possible pre-eclampsia. We would cry for our mummy. 'Bugger your mummy,' Ruby would say. She was not a sentimental woman. She used a uniquely Anglo-Indian word to express her displeasure, her impatience. Oh-*Hoh*. She made curries that shone like copper with ghee. She too softened with age. She was a lovely old lady. I was very sad when she died.

What do I remember most about her?

The way she sat, still and straight-backed, her eyes full of untold stories, her hands in her lap, twiddling and twiddling and twiddling her thumbs.

I still had one grandparent left. The one I knew the least. Ellen, my nana in Kidderminster. Ellen was my mother's real mother. Albert had kept my mother from

Ellen from the age of four. They made their reunion when my mother was twenty-three, when she had just become a mother herself. Ellen was brittle with trauma and sharp with resentment. Her silver hair was cropped short and she wore pale blue NHS spectacles. There was no rapport between my mother and her mother. They were still feeling their way in this strange new union. Ellen was not Anglo-Indian, she was of Scottish descent, but she had kept her Indian accent from her years in India. We didn't see her very often. She died two weeks after my own mother died, another Alzheimer's ending in another old people's home. I was thirty-six.

What do I remember most about her?

The smell of fat, buttery parathas slowly cooking in a heavy frying pan, the anticipation, the honey drizzled over as a treat.

So now I am forty and I have no grandparents, all of those distant, damaged, unknowable people have gone. And what have I taken from them? I have my pale skin, my very English aquiline nose, yet something slightly, indefinably foreign about me. I have a taste for curry, a love of old English houses, a streak of creativity, a deep nostalgic yearning for things I can't quite describe. I am a mongrel girl, full of odd blood and broken histories. When I think of my grandparents I think of over-heated houses and eye-catching ornaments, things we weren't to touch, places we weren't to go, odd-smelling crockery, squash with bits at the bottom, garish wallpaper, huge saucepans of curry, knuckles of meat, damp linoleum, best behaviour, book tokens, poppies on Remembrance Day, the cold marble floors of a Spanish apartment, separate bedrooms, gravelled driveways, the acid colour of Anglo-Indian interiors, white spirits and a squeeze of lime in a heavy tumbler, a Bedlington terrier through a car window: I think of a fusty, tasselled, buttoned-up England that was fading away and a bright, modern multicultural England that was just beginning.

So thank you Jack, Doreen, Albert, Ruby and Ellen, thank you for being my grandparents and for being the five parts of the jigsaw that have made me what I am today. I was not close to any of you, but you are all here, living on inside me, your smells, your opinions, your traditions, your voices, your vices, your histories and your blood. I am proud to be a part of you.

I am proud of my grandparents.

Lisa Jewell is a bestselling novelist, whose books include Ralph's Party, 31 Dream Street *and* The Truth About Melody Browne.

Joel Joffe

My maternal grandmother had no formal education and grew up in a very poor family with ten sisters where, in order to survive, you had to make the best of all opportunities.

She used to look after my siblings and me when our parents were away on holiday. On one occasion our German shepherd proudly returned from an expedition with a chicken in his mouth, almost certainly purloined from a neighbour's chicken coop. We children wondered whether it would be better to surreptitiously return the corpse or apologise profusely as we openly returned it, or do something else. We decided to refer the matter to our granny who seemed in no way perturbed and said she would handle it. That night we had delicious roast chicken for dinner!

On another occasion, my father arrived home with a painting by a well-known South African artist. Granny did not like the look of one man on this painting and made clear her disapproval. My parents went away on holiday, Granny spent a week looking after us, and they returned to discover that she had decided to improve the painting by adding a moustache to the face of the man she disliked!

Our Granny was certainly a woman of action.

Lord Joffe's career spans the legal, financial services, health and voluntary sectors. He began as a Human Rights lawyer in South Africa where he defended Nelson Mandela. After moving to the UK he became, among other achievements, a trustee for a number of charities. He was raised to the peerage in 2000.

Martha Kearney

Every day Martha Kearney walked through the streets of Kensington in order to get to the shops. This was not the Kensington of dark red mansion blocks, white stucco villas, antique shops and security-guarded embassies which I pass on the way to the BBC in west London each day. My grandmother, my namesake, lived in Liverpool's Kensington, still nicknamed 'Kenny' and nowadays one of the poorest areas in the country. Her house was on Romilly Street, one of many early Victorian terraces behind the main thoroughfare of the working-class area near the city centre.

By the time I knew Grandma, she was living in a comfortable house in the suburb of Huyton but I was told many family stories about the struggle of their lives in Liverpool during the Depression of the thirties. These anecdotes often took the form of a morality tale to high-light the relative fortune of our modern lives: 'The One Tangerine Christmas', for instance. But all too quickly, in the callous manner of privileged children, we enjoyed teasing my father about the Monty Pythonesque extremes of his childhood.

What saved the Kearneys from the abject poverty of so many in the area was the entrepreneurial spirit of my grandmother. Martha learned about business from her brother, W.G. Thomas, who had begun with a stall in St John's Market where the families of the journalists Anne Robinson and Gillian Reynolds also had businesses. W.G. ended up with three greengrocers' shops stretching as far away as Chester and family mythology has it that he was the first man to import bananas into Liverpool.

As a young woman, my grandmother opened her own enterprise, a sweetshop on Great Homer Street. Her cunning business plan was to sell cut-price cigarettes, which she bought from a friendly newsagent and smuggled down the street hidden under the mattress of the baby's pram. There must always have been a baby as she had seven children in all (the eldest Arthur died). Despite that large family, she carried on working, which made her unique on Romilly Street. The sweetshop struggled, however, and had to close after a young man ran off with the week's takings. Undeterred, Martha began again with a cake stall in Birkenhead Market and ended up with five stalls, which she handed on to her sons.

I have a photograph of her by the stall with the title 'M. Kearney'. Looking at that black-and-white image makes me proud of her, that she had the spirit and determination to build up her business in such difficult economic circumstances. She also encouraged my father to go to grammar school and on to Cambridge, which has meant my own life has been so much easier than that of my namesake. My only regret is wounding her by drawing an unfortunate comparison. For a child like me growing up in Sussex, an old lady with a hairnet and Northern accent conjured up only one image. I told my lovely warm grandma that she looked like Ena Sharples from *Coronation Street*. That's another Kearney family story which I still haven't lived down.

Martha Kearney is a broadcaster and journalist. She is the main presenter of BBC Radio 4's lunchtime news programme The World at One.

Ann Keen

My granddad was the image of Nikita Khrushchev to look at. My main childhood memories of him were his wonderful shiny head and kind, round face. He was always encouraging me to do new things, especially exercises. He would do a big display and his finale was to count how many times he could touch his toes. I had to keep count, usually up to a hundred. His face would get redder and redder and then it would be my turn but he always beat me. He would end by saying how fit he was.

Most importantly, Granddad had a wonderful garden shed. In this shed he would mend the hole in my shoe, teach me how to repair a puncture and if any of my toys were broken he would always seem to make them work again. All this and much more happened with the help of the tins that contained all sorts of bits and pieces, the shelves laden with pots, the tools and all the smells of his magic shed. However, there is one memory that remains more painful. When a very loose baby tooth was causing me great distress he became my dentist and appeared with a pair of pliers from the shed. My mum told me to grip her apron and with one quick yank, the tooth was in my hand ready for the tooth fairy. Now, as the Health Minster with responsibility for dentistry, I have often thought of my first TV interview when I was asked for my comments on the man who had recently claimed that he had had no alternative but to remove his own teeth with a pair of pliers. I decided it would be unprofessional to appear to empathise! I still have the cobbler's last as a memory of him but no trace of the pliers!

It will be no surprise that I was in the Brownies and every year on the eve of Remembrance Sunday he would show me how to polish my badge and shoes while he polished his medals and we practised marching and saluting in the back kitchen. On Sunday morning we would march to the Remembrance Service at Hawarden and show respect at the Cenotaph. I often wonder what he would think if he knew I was now the president of the Chiswick branch of the Royal British Legion and have the privilege of laying the wreath on its behalf. I never fail to think of him each year I attend in my official capacity. I doubt, however, if I keep to Granddad's standards of 'shoulders back, arms straight' but I always make sure my shoes shine!

When Granddad Tom Hughes retired from Shotton Steelworks, he became keeper of Ewloe Castle – a magical place, especially to a small girl like me, who regularly appeared there dressed as a cowgirl. I would go every weekend it was open and throughout the school summer holidays and especially on Good Friday with all my friends. We would take sandwiches and a pop bottle, which we would fill with water from the natural spring. Because I was 'special', I was allowed to go in the keeper's hut where the ticket books were kept and also a tin with cake and there would be a teapot and sometimes I could have cake and tea.

It was normal in those days for three generations to live together. One night my mum asked me to go upstairs to check if my granddad wanted a cup of tea. When I asked him he didn't answer so I told Mum he was asleep. Later that night everyone was crying and no one would tell me why. The next day I was sent away with my younger brother. I never saw Granddad again. But I will always remember the magic of him as my cobbler, keeper of the castle, my special friend and my very first dentist.

Ann Keen MP represents the Brentford and Isleworth constituency in west London and is the Parliamentary Under-Secretary of State for Health Services.

Lorraine Kelly

My granny Margaret Kelly is eighty-eight years old and lives in Rutherglen just outside Glasgow. She is small and slim with cheekbones that could slice bread, and although her dark hair is white now, she still looks decades younger than her years and is as sharp as a tack.

She still goes on the bus twice a week to the bingo and can easily fill in half a dozen cards at the same time, whereas I would struggle to cope with marking down the numbers of just one single card.

My granny has had a hard life, but she has never lost her sense of humour.

She brought up four kids with my granda Danny: my dad John, my uncle Bille and my aunties Lydia and Carol, and she lost four more to childhood diseases that rampaged through the overcrowded tenements in the Gorbals.

There was never enough money and she remembers that everyone left their doors open because no one had anything worth stealing.

Their tenement flat was just a room and kitchen with everyone crowded into the one bedroom. The toilet was outside and shared by all the other families in the close. Everyone was in the same boat and just got on with living check by jowl.

When I was a little girl I used to love going to my granny's. I was allowed to stay up and watch TV late at night, curled up on the sofa with my aunties and a big bag of boiled sweeties.

I used to love rummaging through her cupboards and finding old biscuit tins with stern-looking Scottish soldiers in kilts on the lid. Inside would be lots of old photographs of generations of Kellys and some of my dad as a wee grumpy boy.

My granny said he cried for the first two years of his life and the hospital were glad to see the back of her first-born when she took him home.

My granny Kelly cooks real traditional Scottish food like Scotch broth and ribs and cabbage, but her triumph is a massive clootie dumpling. The magnificent pudding is the size and shape of a massive pumpkin and stuffed with fruit, nuts, cinnamon and silver sixpences. It was wrapped in a pillowcase and boiled in water for hours on end. The smell of the spices was just wonderful. I would always get a massive slab to take home with me but I would scoff it all before I got out the door.

Sometimes when we visited my granny was in bed with the lights off and the curtains drawn, suffering one of her horrible migraine attacks, but usually she would be in the kitchen making endless ups of tea and coffees for all the family that came visiting and rustling up grills and bacon in her 'magic' frying pan. She used to produce food at an extraordinary rate. I've never known a quicker cook.

Even though I didn't have my daughter Rosie until I was thirty-six, my mum and dad married very young, when they were eighteen. This means my daughter has young grandparents and also a fit and energetic great-granny.

When I was researching my family tree as part of a feature for *GTV*, I had to interview my granny. She was the kind of interviewee that makes you want to burst out cheering – funny, interesting, entertaining.

She was an enormous help when I was writing my autobiography – providing me with lots of background and also some cracking old photos.

She is modest and rather shy, but the absolute salt of the earth.

I hope I look half as good, and have all my marbles just like she does when I reach my eighties.

Lorraine Kelly is a journalist and presenter.

18 Random Memories of My Grandparents

Annie Lennox

My father's father's name was Archibald King Lennox. He was the youngest of six brothers, and lived to the ripe old age of ninety-nine, just missing out on a full century by a mere six months.

Including Archibald, three of my grandparents lived into their nineties. Each one of them was quite distinctive in their own particular way. Having been brought up in the Edwardian era, they had a clearly defined sense of values, firmly underpinned by a stoically enduring Scots work ethic. They lived through two world wars, and had a direct experience of the hardship and struggle which characterised that time.

The two sides of my family were distinctly different. My mother's family came from the countryside, and were traditional conservatives, with a small 'c', while the Lennox's from the town were politically proactive socialist/trade unionists. My mother's mother and father met at Balmoral castle, where my grandmother was the head dairymaid, and my grandfather, William Ferguson, was a gamekeeper.

They were both accustomed to working for the aristocracy, and held a certain sense of respect and loyalty towards them. They knew their 'place', and had no issue with it, while the Lennox side of the family were keenly aware of Karl Marx, the Soviet revolution and the rights of the working man. So there was a kind of tacit schism between both sides of my family tree.

I can't say that any of them were tactile or emotionally demonstrative. It just wasn't the done thing to behave that way, so I grew up to be mildly allergic to open displays of affection.

My grandparents came from a generation where children were more 'seen' than 'heard', so I used to spend a lot of time listening to conversations. I have snippets of memories from the past that still inform my present-day.

Here is a random selection of eighteen memories:

1. The deliciously comforting smell of home-made raspberry jam wafting through the house, as it simmered on the hob in my grandmother's kitchen.
2. A white 1930's china tea service, with tea cups, saucers and square side plates, decorated in vivid orange and green flower patterns.
3. The craggy surface of the back of my grandfather's neck, crisscrossed like a sun weathered map, defining the years of a lifetime spent outdoors on heather moors and hillsides.
4. The splendid tweed suits he wore, with matching caps, waistcoats, plus fours and brown leather brogues.

5   Lighting paraffin lamps on dark winter's nights, as there was no electricity in the house.

6   Digging for a treasure of new potatoes in the back garden.

7   The mildly gruesome sight of my grandmother wringing a chicken's neck, and the resultant acrid smell of singed feathers as she plucked and prepared the carcass for the dinner table .

8   A honey-coloured ferret called Jockie, that I used to to try to communicate with by scraping the cage wire of his wooden hutch until he made a playfully skittish appearance. This outward "cuteness" belied a set of razor-sharp teeth, that could bite off your fingertip if you weren't careful.

9   Carefully collecting warm newly-laid eggs from underneath the hens.

10 The cosily pungent smell of hay in the chicken shed.

11 The first time I ever tasted wild salmon, caught directly from the river Spey, and brought home as pink cutlets wrapped in newspaper. I've never had a culinary experience like it since.

12 Sitting on a patch of warm earth underneath a bird net, selecting the biggest strawberries I could find.

13 The heavenly indulgence of lying on my grand-mother's bed, reading library books for as long as I liked, with no interference from anyone else at all.

14 Archibald's jaunty hat collection, and his novel way of re-inventing anything that could be recycled.

15 His greenhouse, and the wonderfully edgy smell of sun-ripened tomatoes.

16 My grandmother's longstanding patience with his somewhat overbearing attitudes and longwinded opinions.

17 Sunday suppers with ham salads and pale yellow "salad cream" (which I thought was very sophisticated).

18 Being taken for a ride on the back of Archibald's motorbike down to the beach boulevard and back.

These are just glimpses of memories. I go back to them, or they come back to me in day dreams. A sentimental part of me wishes I could go back there again, but time has a curious habit of marching onwards.

Annie Lennox, born on Christmas day in 1954, is one of the UK's most recognisable and successful artists. Internationally acclaimed, her award-winning career has spanned three decades. An official ambassador for Amnesty International, Oxfam and Nelson Mandela's 46664 campaign, she continuously supports countless charitable organisiations – www.annielennoxsing.com

Kathy Lette

My maternal Grandma was in her anecdotage… but from about the age of *six*. She bequeathed to my mother and me a love of language, jokes and, yes, puns. My grandma – crossword fiend, scrabble champ, anagram-queen and walking thesaurus – was my favourite pun-pal.

A born storyteller, Mary Grieve lived for one hundred and one years. At the time of her death her life had spanned almost half of Australia's European history. To her family she was a neverending source of quality yarns about her adventurous past. Tales of bare-footed five-mile treks to bush schools which made us weep; encounters with snakes – both slithering and two-legged (they lost their dairy farm to debt collectors during the Depression) which made us fume; raft trips up the shark-infested Georges River, leaving us squirming in terror. As an accomplished antic-collector, no doubt these tales were all highly embellished but they were also bum-numbingly entertaining. Young and old, we perched for hours at her feet.

She never read but regaled her eight grandchildren with a wealth of stories. There were traditional tales, Aboriginal dreamtime mythology, folklore, legends, Bible stories, fairy stories – all told with a cackling sense of mischievous humour. ('Why are there no more fairy tales in the library?' I remember her chuckling to me, 'Because they ran out of elf space.') From the heroics of King Arthur and his Genevieve ('Arthur any more at home like you?') and the exploits of Sinbad the Sailor (a 'crewed business') to Zeus sending Atlas off to hold up the world ('Atlas we are alone!'). From Eve eating the apple ('cores and effect, dear children') to the saga of her Norwegian father's shipwreck rounding Cape Horn, we kids sat, rapt.

It was obvious that my Grandma had grown up on a dairy as the woman could milk more pathos out of 'The Little Match Girl' or drama from 'Daniel in the Lion's Den' than any Shakespearean actor, 'No holes Bard'. (Actually, she *didn't* say that, but she *should* have – what can I say? It's genetic.) My grandma loved the English language and used it with grace and facility. She taught me the longest word in the dictionary – 'antidisestablishmentarianism' – and the most useful word for an author 'lexiphanic' – given to the use of pretentious terminology, such as the word lexiphanic.

A schoolteacher by profession, she amazed her liberated granddaughters with the fact that once married, she was forced to resign because the Married Teachers' Act forbade married women to teach. Years later when she had five young children, she was called back to service during the Second World War. After decades of permanent teaching, she continued as a supply teacher well into her seventies. At her retirement party, many of her ex-students, now retired themselves, turned up to thank her.

Many virtues were reflected in her life: loyalty, honesty, duty, courage, kindness, compassion. ('We all have our foibles,' she once told me, 'Aesop was famous for his.') But above all, she possessed a steadfast faith.

Grandma was no wowser though and at our many family gatherings she was always ready with a corny joke. She once asked, 'What is pink and wrinkly and hangs out your grandfather's underpants?'

We teenagers, frozen with horror that such a risqué joke could emanate from our very proper Grandmother, could think of only one possible, blush-inducing answer.

'Do you give up?' she twinkled. 'Your *grandmother*, of course!'

Mary Grieve, my beloved one hundred and one-year-old gran – a great storyteller, whose very best and most astounding story was her own.

To conclude, I'm sure she wouldn't mind if, in her humorous honour, I told you that her jokes were like her Nordic eyes, blue as the sea – only cornea.

Kathy Lette first achieved succès de scandale as a teenager with the novel Puberty Blues, *made into a major film. Now published in more than 100 countries, she has written ten internationally bestselling novels including* How To Kill Your Husband *and* Mad Cows. *Her latest novel is* To Love, Honour and Betray – Till Divorce Us Do Part.

Catherine Lockerbie

My grandmother was the no-nonsense angel of woolly jumpers and wickedly good shortbread. 'Grandmother' is in truth too grand and posh a name for her. She was always just Granny, the only one of my grandparents still alive as I was growing up, gawky and bookish.

Her visits brought oblong biscuit tins and enfolding wool. I look at photos of me as a little blonde tomboy in Fair Isle sweaters. Fair Isle! Only Granny could have knitted those.

Born in Dumfries in 1909, she belonged to a far harsher world. Her son, my father, was the first of his family to educate himself into the middle class. His mother scrubbed other people's floors at brutal hours of the dawn. I could barely envisage her life and she never told me – she just, in my limited, selfish, childhood consciousness, baked and knitted, things which barely happened in our own family life. She was sharp and soft at the same time – no namby-pamby nonsense, or molly-coddling affection – but we did get those melting, mouth-cuddling biscuits.

And I got my jumper. Many of them, but one in particular.

At school I was clever and hopeless. I could answer all the brainy questions but couldn't stick balsa wood together satisfactorily and was woefully hopeless at sewing and knitting. (I loved books above all and it was tricky to read and wield knitting needles at the same time). Required to knit an entire jumper at school at the tender age of ten, I struggled pathetically. The intended garment was to be pale blue, with dark blue for the neck and the cuffs – and I worked my way wonkily through one little bit of the back. Granny moved in to the rescue. I don't remember the exact moment she briskly whisked it from me but I do remember the glorious moment I got it back – complete! Beautifully knitted sleeves, front, everything, except for a few curiously crooked rows of purl and plain. My teacher was suitably impressed. (Cheating? What cheating?)

I have it to this day, a specific memento of her, strangely undestroyed by the moths, which have assiduously chomped all the other ancient woollies. My blue jumper lives at the bottom of the wardrobe of my son – her great-grandson whom she briefly cradled before she died – so much loved, imperfect, perfect.

Catherine Lockerbie has been a teacher, broadcaster, journalist, literary editor and director of the Edinburgh International Book Festival, one of the world's largest celebrations of words and ideas. She has been awarded five honorary doctorates for her work.

Family Values
Jean Loudon

What does it feel like to be a grandparent? Or a grand-child for that matter? I've been thinking about grandparents for weeks now, and it is a bit like being on a see-saw. As a grandchild I look back on my Victorian-born grandparents, but as a grandparent I look forward to my ten grandchildren, born from 1979 to 2006. So it is a two-headed process.

An only child, I grew up feeling deprived of family, uneasy as to what family meant, unsure that I had the right sort of family, much as I loved my parents. My best friend had lots of brothers and sisters, and grandparents living in an enormous house in the Sussex countryside. I stayed there once when I was nine, being driven down in an open Bentley, about seven of us, and the grandfather at the end of it was a huddle in a chair. I loved books about large happy families, wanted children, and when my children were grown up was so happy to have grand-children. I still am.

So much is talked about Victorian family values, and

looking at my own family I think much of it is guff. My father kept well away – and kept me away, too – from his family, though he did help them out quite a lot financially, and I know almost nothing about them. There are family values for you.

My mother's parents were much more a part of my life. My grandmother Cecil Sowerby was born in London in 1866, the youngest of six girls and a boy, and I remember her telling me she was her father's pet. Her father was very musical, had been a choirboy in the Temple Church in the City, and worked for Barclays Bank. She said all her other relations were botanists or conchologists. Her great-grandfather James Sowerby produced the 36-volume *Sowerby's English Botany*, and there is a Sowerby's Whale in the Natural History Museum in London. While my mother's father, Arthur Dixon (an artist and jeweller), was in many ways a solitary man, Cecil certainly had a strong sense of family, which included parties, clothes, music, and enjoying company all her life.

As a child, Cecil spent some months in a Convent of the Sacred Heart School but hated it, and was allowed to come home. She trained as an artist, and as she had cousins in France her parents let her go to Paris to study. I never saw anything she had drawn or painted. Later, she was governess to Christabel and Sylvia Pankhurst, who remembered being taken by her to the British Museum.

What I remember is her belief. Cecil was always religious. She recalled going to chapel with her nurse, and in later life she joined the Society of Friends – Quakers – though she stipulated that she be allowed to continue to take communion in the Church of England. I don't know if she ever did.

My grandfather Arthur Dixon was born in London in 1872, and went to the Slade School of Art at University College, London. I remember my uncle Charles describing to me the rush when Arthur's paintings were being prepared for submission to the Royal Academy. I don't know how often they were accepted. The oil paintings I saw were fairly conventional, touched by pre-Raphaelitism. There is at least one in the Walker Art Gallery in Liverpool. I remember Cecil describing how before they were married in 1899, she and Arthur would, when travelling by tram, play chess together, only moving the pieces when the tram stopped. A few years after they married they left London and lived in Sussex with their two small children. She wrote in her Bible the date of birth of her daughter Elizabeth – my mother – and then of her son Charles, described as 'first son'. There weren't any more. Those Edwardian years sounded tranquil enough.

However, by the time I knew them my maternal grandparents were leading very separate lives in a house in Berkhamsted, a town well stocked with retired army and colonial service families. My grandparents were liberal, artistic; army people were not their sort of people. My question now is not what my grandparents were like, but why they were so distant from each other, which is not something I ever considered as a child. Separate bedrooms. It's just the way it was.

Cecil stayed in the house, though made forays up to London to do voluntary social work somewhere in Bethnal Green. She also did embroidery, wool work on cotton or blankets, and some weaving for her own pleasure. A blanket Cecil embroidered has been used by her great-great-granddaughters, and one of them will inherit it. I never saw her read a book, and I think she irritated my mother, who was scholarly. But she was good-hearted and hospitable. When staying with my grandparents in 1939, I noticed that she had a very wide circle of friends, many of them very young, who would visit in the evening, to talk and sing round the piano. She was clearly popular.

Arthur had the studio at home, which was really a large wooden hut that half-filled the garden. You first had to telephone the studio from the house by cranking the handle of an intercom telephone arrangement to see if it was all right to visit. Cecil was never, ever, allowed in the studio, though Arthur's good friends the Misses Ethel and Hope Henderson were. To get in you had to press down on a small piece of wood that was under the threshold and then the door would open. The first part of the studio contained two life-sized model figures on which clothes could be draped, and were usually covered in cotton sheeting. There was also a quarter-sized billiard table. Arthur played against himself and my mother claimed he cheated. The second and larger part beyond a dividing curtain contained a small easel, but mainly chests of shallow drawers with stones and rings and brooches in them, and a worktop with a Bunsen burner. The jewellery he made was firmly in the Arts and Crafts tradition, semi-precious stones set in oxidised silver. They are very distinctive and although not hallmarked I can easily recognise them and have twice been able to tell people who made their rings. Evelyn Waugh, writing in his 1918 diary clearly liked them too, as well as a dance in the house when Cecil played the piano. Arthur taught me how to make pendants and set stones, and was very patient. There was a bench covered in something embroidered by Cecil, and the unbound first editions of Bernard Shaw's plays. It was a room that entranced me.

What did I mean to them? My grandmother fussed over me; I can see now she wanted to be loved, wanted demonstrative affection which on the whole she didn't get from me. She wanted to be called Cecil, not Granny, because I had always called my grandfather Arthur, and I suspect she felt out of it. I feel sorry as a child for not really loving her. I did love Arthur, so did my mother, and he loved us back, always. But I don't think he had a sense of family as something all-embracing, though I think Cecil probably did.

Still, I didn't understand why they lived as they did until my mother got an inoperable cancer. She said then she had always meant to tell me the story of her life, and she began, but actually only told me the story, or part of the story, of her parents' lives. And the separateness of two people who had a good deal in common – pacifists, vegetarians, frugal, true children of the Arts and Crafts era – became clear. Before the First World War, then living in a house designed by Cecil's architect brother-in-law, Arthur fell in love with the woman next door. When it all came out, the next-door family moved. Divorce was ruled out because of the children, though they seemed to have known what was going on; my mother said she liked the woman concerned very much – at the time better than her own mother, is my guess – while her brother sided with his mother. So the family was split emotionally. How Arthur coped I've no idea. Cecil said it was the worst night of her life, and it took its toll of them all.

So, in my eighties, what is it like to be a grandparent now? I still feel sorry that I didn't pay more attention to my grandparents when I was grown up. In contrast, I am slightly surprised, and immensely pleased, that our grandchildren send us emails, come and see us and bring their friends too. Most importantly, I see the lines of communication in the family widen, become more lateral, between parents, aunts and uncles, siblings and cousins. Which is what I always hoped would happen.

Jean Loudon was born in 1926, evacuated during the war to Canada, and has a degree from King's College, London. She is married to the medical historian and etcher Irvine Loudon, and has three surviving daughters, two sons, and ten grandchildren.

Photographs
Mary Loudon

At home, I have a lot of black-and-white photographs of my extended family on the wall. The family is very big and the photographs give me a feeling of safety and continuity. Images of my husband and small daughters on the beach, my sisters looking sassy, and my parents in a car with a starter-motor handle, contend with those of my brothers posing in wraparound shades, and my nephews, beaming, in transit; and then, like a pause for breath in the midst of this collective clamour for attention, are two photographs not vying for it at all.

In the first, taken around 1910, a woman of sixty, encased in stiff Edwardian silk but with a cat on her lap and more than half a smile playing around the corners of her handsome mouth, gazes easily into the camera lens. She is wearing a monogrammed signet ring on her little finger. I wear it on the third finger of my right hand, and sometimes it is a little loose, so I surmise from that that she had considerably larger hands than I do, and was therefore somewhat taller. I share her three first initials, which is, I think, why the ring came to me.

In the second photograph, taken in around 1875, a woman who was the contented cat-lover's exact contemporary, was photographed to celebrate her engagement. The diamond engagement ring she wore now takes turns on the same finger of mine that often bears the signet ring of the woman whose son was to marry her daughter.

I think my paternal great-grandmothers would have had difficulty imagining that.

My paternal grandfather, Andrew, inherited his mother's love of cats: a GP-surgeon, he knew every cat in the parish by name. My father's first emergency surgical procedure, including the administration of chloroform, was carried out at as a small boy at his father's side, on a cat that had been run over and badly injured outside the surgery. The operation was successful, and fascinating for a boy who was to follow his father into medicine, but my father had no interest in cats. It was a dog he wanted and it was a dog that my grandfather, selflessly, for he had no interest in dogs, bought for my father. My father has not been dogless since.

My only memory of Andrew is animal related. I was less than two, and staying with him at Berryhill, my grandparents' house. It had a lawn sloping into a wood, through which steam trains occasionally passed on a branch line. I loved that place and daydream about it often. Shaving before his bathroom mirror one sunny morning, observed closely by me, he spotted a hedgehog out of the window. 'We'd better go and feed it,' he said; which we did, with bread and milk in a saucer.

Andrew loved horses as well as hedgehogs, cats, and the birds he used to watch. After he qualified in medicine in Edinburgh he joined the Territorials, at least in part because he wanted to learn to ride. When the First World War broke out, he was given a milkman's dray horse, Billy, and he and Billy were sent to France where Andrew was in charge of a casualty clearing station, positioned just behind the front line. It was very dangerous and he was one of the few to survive, though no one knows whether Billy did. A photograph of Andrew with Billy, taken in Armentières in April 1915, is on my father's wall. It must have been one of the last taken in that period: in 1915 photography was banned at the front, but by then Andrew had already amassed a great many pictures. He later deposited them with the Imperial War Museum in London, where they remain.

I have a beautiful Gladstone bag of Andrew's, initialled on one side, a classic doctor's bag from another era. As a child, I sat on the eighteenth-century dining chairs that came from his family and ate from his silver, and now I wear his mother's signet ring. I live among his lovely things, but what I really possess of him is not silver or gold, not wisdom passed down, not even hearsay or anecdote, nor history brought one step closer with a leather bag of scalpels used in the field where brave men suffered and died. What matters to me is the hedgehog, the saucer of milk, and the scent of shaving soap.

There are photographs of Andrew on my wall, looking staggeringly handsome at forty, sixty and eighty. Morag – the woman he was to marry, and whose real name was Sarah – is there, too, looking pensive in her thirties, though she is not placed next to him. She is beside my other grandmother, Elizabeth, pictured at around twenty, and my mother at fourteen: I hung them together because in all three photographs their heads are turned in exactly the same three-quarter profile, which is pleasing to the eye.

'You,' Morag said to me, often, 'are as stubborn as an ass.' She brooked no nonsense from her youngest grandchild, but was patient with me, too. She had a gift for entertaining small children and would play tirelessly without props of any kind. Usually the games took place on her lap in a large armchair by a window. My favourite game was Pecking Birds: she held out the palms of her hands filled with imaginary crumbs and the birds – my fingers – would peck until the crumbs were gone. Then we would swap. Morag's hands were large and broad, her lap ample, and she smelled of Pears soap. Except when in bed, or for very formal occasions, I never saw her dressed in anything other than soft navy blue wool skirts and cardigans with a crisp white linen blouse, and a brooch at her throat. Her skin was cashmere soft, and her white hair soft also, swept back into a generous bun and secured with two tortoiseshell combs. I don't recall ever seeing it down, or being given permission to brush it. I saw it loose only when she was in bed, ill, in the few days before she died.

Morag was the one person I regarded as a proper grandparent. She lived with us for several months at the end of her life and in that time we loved one another and argued vigorously, which I am certain we both enjoyed. Born in 1883, Morag grew up under Queen Victoria: when she died aged nearly ninety in 1973 she was a Victorian still. I was six then, infused with her recollections of nineteenth-century nursery games but with older siblings already in Bob Dylan's grip. I was watching *Shari Lewis and Lambchop* on the television when my mother came to tell me that Morag had died. In furious shock and denial I hit her before bursting into tears.

Morag's death was my original great loss, her funeral my first. I wasn't prepared for the disappearance of her coffin beyond the curtains at the crematorium: they shut slightly later than they should have done and I watched, appalled, as the casket was lowered electronically into a hole that was not a grave but a place from which it would be retrieved, so that it could be burned, with Morag in it. I wasn't happy with that idea at all, and the image of the vanishing coffin haunted me for years to come. I can recall it perfectly still, aged forty-two.

Other funerals since have been worse but none such a shock. Grief was a blow, too. Months after my grandmother's death, my father found me sobbing in the bathroom in a comforting spot between the radiator and the laundry basket.

'What's the matter?' he asked.

'I just miss Morag,' I said, and I did.

Morag and Andrew were easy to comprehend. Their lives were straightforward. Morag enjoyed children; Andrew liked to fish and walk in the Scottish mountains. There was nothing rash or dangerous about their personalities and while they lacked neither depth nor courage they did not actively seek out life's risky perimeters.

The same could not be said of my mother's father Frederick. In a photograph taken in 1937, he is walking across a London square, wearing a belted raincoat and a Fedora hat, lavish around the brim. It is obvious from the photograph that the camera was tilted, because he is listing at around sixty degrees. A flock of pigeons is fanning skywards from the ground immediately behind him, and his manner – self-assurance so complete that it borders on self-satisfied – would render perfectly reasonable any suggestion that they are ascending to order. They are there, it seems, purely to glamorise my grandfather's passage across one of Europe's great capitals, and better to reflect his own sense of momentum at a time when Europe was accelerating towards disaster.

Frederick, who was Professor of German at King's College, London, was always known as Bimbo. With an English father and German mother, he was educated in Germany and in November 1914, aged seventeen, was invited to join the German Army. He declined and was punished with internment in a German Prisoner of War camp. The youngest prisoner there, he was nicknamed Bimbo, a diminutive of Bambino. The German authorities did not release him until the winter of 1918: however, in that time, unwittingly they had equipped an ambitious young man with ammunition that was seriously to back-fire upon them later. Four years in the company of native German speakers and political prisoners placed Bimbo in an ideal environment to develop the linguistic polish and skill for secrecy that were the bases of his Second World War career – as a spy for MI5, working at Bletchley Park in England.

What I know about Bimbo I might know about a character from one of John Le Carré's novels but I never actually knew him. He bequeathed to me, like my grandfather Andrew, just one vivid memory. Aged less than two, I was sitting on his lap, with loud orchestral music playing on a gramophone nearby. I've no idea what it was but I know he became impatient with me when I objected to its noise and he fed me, from a bag tucked into a bookcase, with pink and white marshmallows. 'These should shut you up,' he announced, correctly.

And that was that. He died shortly afterwards in December 1968 on a park bench in Vienna. A few days later, my step-grandmother had a letter from him, posted on the day he died, in which he explained that he was on his way to visit a friend, who was in bed having had several strokes. He didn't want to be like that, he wrote: he wanted to go out like a light. (Though probably not that very afternoon.) It's only recently that I learned he expired on that bench and not on the ground. It shouldn't make a difference, but for years I'd imagined him flat out in his 1937 raincoat and Fedora, facing skywards, taken aback certainly, but possibly rather pleased about such a neat, quick outcome with more than an edge of drama. Yet I suppose the Viennese bench fits well with the hazy subterfuge of Bimbo's later life, for he left behind a number of unanswered questions, including several pertaining to a Swiss bank account in his name. It was allegedly so well stocked that the Trustees of his will were too alarmed, and fiscally too proper, to empty it. Instead, they left it untouched and access to it remains frustratingly, but perhaps appropriately, obscure.

Mystery still surrounds aspects of Bimbo's life, yet he feels more tangible to me than his first wife, Dicky, the grandmother I never met, who died from cancer twelve years before I was born. When I first told my husband that Dicky was known as Dicky, and not by her real name, Elizabeth, he asked what it was about some families that everyone has to have a silly name. He said it reminded him of the *Ripping Yarns* sketch where everyone is called Biffo and Dinghy.

The daughter of artists, Dicky was solitary, scholarly, ascetic and practical: my mother once remarked that despite her atheism Dicky would have made an excellent medieval abbess. In fact, she was a child psychotherapist at Guy's Hospital in London, specialising in childhood autism and schizophrenia at a time when many women worked but few had careers. She was a good cook and seamstress and an accomplished gardener. When she felt low or needed to be alone, she liked to go into her garden and dig. Sometimes, when I am pulling up nettles, finding similar restoration in solitary physical exertion, I think of her.

I cannot picture Dicky clearly, though. I gaze at her three-quarter profile on the wall, or the photograph in which she kneels before my one-year-old mother in play. In another photograph she is older, looking slightly startled, holding one of the cigarettes that helped to kill her. And I see her but I don't recognise her. I try to imagine the manifestations of her character; in short, the things she did. She and my grandfather were certainly not short of money but she was devout in her frugality, and economics means nothing to people of that ilk. When visiting my parents she would habitually open windows, then leave the rooms in which she had done so. My father, seething, would close them after her. Cold, for him, was intolerable. Cold, for her, was a matter of principle.

I knew Morag well as a child. Andrew and Bimbo left me with one memory each but they were strongly indicative of character. Andrew's kindliness towards animals, and his instinct for gently amusing a young child was clear in the feeding of the hedgehog. Bimbo's irascibility was memorable and the dominant nature of his personality embodied by the over-loud music. I must say that I'm relieved, in retrospect, about his marshmallow bribes, offered as a highly effective substitute for the power of reason. In a household where several languages were spoken, politics discussed, and visitors to the house – or so it seems – were invariably well connected or illustrious, it is reassuring to know that even with the mantle of his OBE and his success and his money, my grandfather was undone by a bog-standard toddler's tantrum.

When it comes to Dicky, however, I feel deprived of her in ways I do not of the others. I wonder often what I might have inherited from her, for she and I share little, it seems. In fact, I mostly consider the qualities and quirks she possessed in terms of the ones I do not. She feels historical to me in a way that my other grandparents don't and I have always felt that if I had just one memory of an event that was hers and mine alone then I would understand her; and I would exist for her, too, which of course I never did. A hedgehog, some marshmallows and the scent of Pears soap are attached to people who touched me, and I think of Andrew, Morag and Bimbo as three separate but distinct pillars. Dicky is the indistinct fourth pillar, so far away as to feel imaginary. She upholds and contains a quarter of my genetic inheritance but she will never have any immediacy. And for that, more than half a century after her death, I am sorry.

Mary Loudon is the prize-winning author of four books: her latest book, Relative Stranger, *has been published world-wide to enormous acclaim. Mary has written widely, and is a regular radio broadcaster. She is married with three daughters, and lives in Oxfordshire and the Wye Valley.*

My Grandmother's Dressing Table

Elsa McAlonan

I have my grandmother to thank for my life-long love affair with beauty products. She was always very beautiful even as an old lady in her eighties, with a white curly perm, she still had a girlish sparkle that belied her years. In her youth, she had thick, long chestnut hair that hung in big, fat waves down her back and smiling eyes, a clear aquamarine shade, which kept their colour almost up until the day she passed away, aged eighty-four.

My grandmother had more access to beauty products than most women. Her husband, my grandfather Thomas Burrows, had a chemist's shop in Beeston, Nottinghamshire. He sold beauty creams and cosmetics and during the war, my mother remembers him sitting for hours at the kitchen table making up 'Liquid Stockings', which looked like bottles of gravy, but were welcomed by all the women who were stationed at the nearby army depot.

As a young child, I don't remember Grandma wearing much make-up, but I do remember her sitting at her large, Edwardian dressing table, which stood proudly in front of her bedroom window. Her dressing table was the most exciting place in the world to me, with its mysterious bottles and jars and little blue-and-white patterned pots, containing all sorts of secrets, though in reality probably just held hairgrips.

Curiosity always got the better of me, as I opened the little drawers, expecting to find hidden treasures, but only finding a large fluffy powder puff and the tiniest little book of tissue thin paper – Papier Poudre – that she had used for years to blot any trace of a shiny nose but which I had always secretly thought would make a better dolly's notebook.

There was a tiny blue cardboard box that contained Bourjois blusher – a little bit of rouge, as she called it – which she applied to the apples of her cheeks with cotton wool to give her pale skin a peachy glow.

In the fifties she wore foundation – Revlon's Touch & Glow and Max Factor's Crème Puff – and stayed loyal to those brands to the day she died. There was a small round white box of Coty loose powder with dandelions painted on it, which I thought was very pretty, and always wished she'd hurry up and use it all, so I could use the box to keep things in.

Grandma used Pond's Cold Cream Cleanser for all her skincare needs and used it for just about everything.

There were no anti-ageing creams or potions, her only advice about avoiding lines and wrinkles was to always protect your face from the sun and to avoid frowning – at all costs.

My grandmother had the most beautiful skin, a soft, velvety complexion that some women would pay hundreds of pounds to achieve these days. Through my work as a beauty writer, I have met many of the world's top facialists, women with 'magic fingers' and waiting lists and highly successful product ranges. One of these skincare queens, Eve Lom, has a world-famous regime based on daily cleansing with an oily cleanser and then rinsing it off several times with a muslin cloth. The Eve Lom Cleanser is a bestseller, adored by celebrities and beauty industry insiders and her flawless complexion is proof that she follows her own tried and tested routine. My grandmother's own cleaning regime involved rubbing in a few dollops of Pond's Cream and removing it with a flannel, soaked in warm water. She would finish it off with a few splashes of cold water and she never, ever used moisturiser.

Nobody in the family ever remembers her wearing any eye make-up, although she would have been able to have her pick of the chemist's shop counters. Her own eye colour was so unusual – you would need coloured contact lenses today to achieve the exact shade of turquoise – that she never needed any eyeshadow or mascara. She wore lipstick – but never in an obvious way.

There was always a well-worn stub of scarlet lipstick in her dressing table drawer, which she applied with her finger, to produce the effect top make-up artists like Bobbi Brown describe today as a 'stain'. Her technique obviously worked a treat as we were never left with red lipstick kisses on our cheeks when we went to visit her.

She never wore perfume, but she always kept a bottle of Yardley's lavender water on her dressing table, which she dabbed on her pulse points on special occasions. Occasionally, if she fancied a change, she would switch to 4711 Eau de Cologne, a scent that reminded her of her own father. He used to put a couple of drops of 4711 on to his freshly laundered handkerchiefs, invigorated by the clean, citrussy scent and ever after, the smell always made her feel close to her father.

Strangely it wasn't either scent that reminds me of my grandmother, decades after she died. Instead the most memorable smell for me was the unmistakable aroma of TCP. She was a germphobic all her life and used to gargle religiously with it every day to keep the germs at bay.

She had an ebony dressing table set that as a child, I was convinced was worth a fortune, with her initial, F, embossed on her hairbrushes, clothes brush and mirror in silver.

My grandmother bought me my first lipstick, as long as I promised not to tell my mother. It was a tiny bullet of Outdoor Girl's Old Wine, which was a wicked, glossy red-black colour and I liked to think smelled of wine as well. It made me feel instantly grown up and quite naughty, so at the age of ten I discovered make-up's magical ability to transform and cheer you up. Several hundred lipsticks later, that feeling has stayed with me ever since.

Recently I was researching on the Internet for my weekly *Daily Mail* beauty column and came across a website which had two whole pages devoted to retro health and beauty products. What's more, all of these products are still going strong and can be easily bought with a couple of clicks. And there they all were – all the secrets of my grandmother's dressing table – Pond's Cold Cream Cleanser, Max Factor's Crème Puff , 4711 Eau de Cologne and even Papier Poudre, all for just a few pounds each.

It's incredible that in an industry worth billions of pounds, these products have not only survived, but have played their part in beautifying generations of women. Perhaps it's because they are all inexpensively priced, or more importantly, perhaps it's because they all did and continue to do exactly what they say they will. Which when it comes to beauty products, really is the only thing we want to know.

Elsa McAlonan is a former editor of Woman's Own *and* Woman's Journal *and now writes a weekly beauty column, Beauty Confidential, for the* Daily Mail.

Grandma Wilma
Richard McCann

We have two children, and one of the most heartbreaking things I am going to have to explain to them is why they don't have a Grandma Wilma. Wilma McCann, my mother, was murdered by the serial killer Peter Sutcliffe a week before my sixth birthday. My wife Helen and I tell our daughter, the eldest, that Grandma Wilma is in heaven and is looking down from above, which was what I was told just after Mum was killed.

We have no doubt that both of them will never forget Grandma Wilma as both of them have been named after a place that has special meaning for us and reminds us of a time when Mum was alive.

One story I will take pleasure in telling our children was of a journey which began back in 2005, which had an incredible and almost spiritual conclusion around fifteen months later. I took Helen, who had just agreed to marry me, to the Isle of Skye to holiday for a week. We decided on the Isle of Skye instead of the continent as we had both fallen in love with the place a couple of months earlier when two of Mum's sisters, who lived in Inverness, had taken us over there to show us where they had all lived in the early sixties. The house by now was an old ruin.

The holiday was incredible and I felt as though we were close to Mum the entire time we were there. On the last day of the holiday we decided to pay one last visit to the place where Mum had lived. As we approached the ruins, on the other side of the loch, I noticed something extraordinary: a great beam of light pierced out of the dark clouds and fell upon a small white croft. I was so amazed by the sight that I stopped my car where it was on the road and took out my camera and snapped a picture of the incredible scene. I intended knocking on the door of the croft, which was around 200 yards from the ruin, to offer the owner a copy of the picture. I would certainly have appreciated a copy if I had lived there. It truly was the kind of thing that postcards are made of. We then drove a few minutes more to the old ruin and took the last few pictures of what was left of the house where my mother had lived all those years ago. It was quite emotional and we never did knock on the door of the croft that had been surrounded by the beams of light. We returned home the next day and I wondered when we might get a chance to visit the place that by now was beginning to mean so much to me.

Around five weeks later I received an email via my website from a man called Dugald Ross. Since writing my first book *Just a Boy* in 2004 I have received emails from all around the world. This one was different. Dugald wrote, telling me that he was writing to me from the house that my mother had lived in when she was a child, on the Isle of Skye. I thought that there must be some mistake having seen the old ruin only weeks earlier. I sent an email back to Dugald asking for a photograph which he sent me the next day. I could not believe it. The house that mum had lived in had not been the ruin at all but the house that I took a picture of surrounded by the beam of light. It was as if Mum had being trying to tell me something, or so I hoped. A few weeks later I visited Skye again, this time visiting the house that Mum had actually lived in. Dugald shared some old memories that he had of my mother.

Helen and I set a date for our wedding – 11 August 2006 – and decided it was time we bought a house together. No sooner had the offer been accepted for a house that we both felt would make a good family home then Helen fell pregnant. The amazing thing was that our baby was due on our wedding day. We were over the moon about being pregnant but a little disappointed that we had to cancel the wedding. One thing I had always wanted was to be married if I ever had children. What we eventually decided to do, without telling any friends or family, was to run away and marry a few weeks before our first child was born. We became Mr and Mrs Richard

McCann on 1 July 2006, Mum's birthday, and on the doorstep of the house that she had lived in. We had no guests and Dugald and his wife Debbie were our witnesses. It was so romantic and it felt as though it was the closest we could get to having my mother at our wedding. Helen looked radiant being so pregnant and the child arrived around six weeks later. She was a healthy girl and we knew immediately what we would call her: Skye McCann, to ensure that she will always remember how significant her Grandma, who she will never meet, was in our choosing of her name. Our son was born the following year and we did not hesitate in choosing his name either. We called him Ellis after Ellishadder, the place in which his Grandma Wilma lived when she was younger and where his mum and dad married on what would have been Grandma Wilma's fifty-ninth birthday.

Richard McCann is a motivational speaker and the author of Just a Boy *and* The Boy Grows Up.

Heather McGregor

My grandmother always made me feel better. She was my mother's mother, and in some ways my mother also; born into a single parent family, we moved to live with my grandparents when I could barely walk, and for the first few years of my life she cared for me. Even when I acquired a loving stepfather, and we moved out, her home was always a refuge. My memories are all of love and warmth, and knowing that if I was ever unwell or unhappy, she would make me feel better. Sitting in her back room, by a solid-fuel Rayburn, eating fish fingers and then being allowed to watch *Blue Peter* on her black-and-white television, are some of my warmest memories of my earliest years.

Sadly my grandmother was crippled with arthritis and died in her early eighties when I was eighteen. But long before she died, she handed to my mother a recipe that had been handed down to her from her grandmother – a hot drink designed to ward off the common cold. Goodness knows if it works or not, but it certainly tastes very nice, and like my grandmother's house and her love, makes me feel better whenever I am a bit under the weather.

My mother, a wonderful grandmother to my children and my sister's, handed down the recipe to me, to share with you. So now we can all feel better.

ELDERBERRY SYRUP

Pick as many ripe elderberries as you wish. Cover with cold water, bring to the boil and simmer for a while. (My grandmother has written here 'stew well', but I think we can interpret that as 'simmer for a while').

When cool, strain. Then, to every pint of liquid add one pound of sugar, twelve cloves, I teaspoon of ginger and 1 teaspoon of cinnamon. Boil (again, I think we can interpret this as 'simmer') for half an hour.

When cool, strain and bottle. To drink, add one tablespoon of liquid to hot water in a glass. Enjoy!

Heather McGregor is the principal shareholder in executive search firm Taylor Bennett and writes the Mrs Moneypenny column in the Financial Times.

Aasia Mahmood

Whenever someone mentions his or her grandfather my thoughts turn to the memories of my maternal grandfather, Colonel Ibrahim Khan or 'Abba Jee' as he was affectionately known by all of his grandchildren. He was everyone's favourite grandparent.

Abba Jee was involved and interested in every aspect of his grandchildren's lives from day one. In fact he was involved in their welfare even before they were born. His moral and practical support was always greatly appreciated by my parents at all occasions but more so during the special occasion of the arrival of a new baby. My grandfather was present at the time of the birth of all five of us brothers and sisters. He even held my mother's hands in the delivery room during the birth of my younger sister. Being a doctor his presence was reassuring and a source of great comfort to my mother. He would help her to shop for baby clothes and other baby paraphernalia. All these tasks around the birth of a child are traditionally performed by grandmothers in Pakistan. As my maternal grandmother had passed away soon after my mother fell pregnant for the first time, Abba Jee took on the dual roles of grandmother and grandfather very successfully and, I think, quite willingly.

He was a very hands-on grandfather. During his stay with us he would help us with our homework, especially in writing up English essays. He told us stories from Greek Mythology and explained their relevance to English literature. He was an avid fan of cricket and we learned much about the game, its history and its famous figures from him. He would regale us with the history of the Ashes, the bodyline Series, and the escapades of Douglas Jardine and Donald Bradman. One of my enduring memories is of Abba Jee, my parents and all of us siblings huddled around a radio listening to live commentary of a Pakistan—England match.

As we grew older and learned about his experiences during the Second World War, we would press Abba Jee to tell us stories from his days as a prisoner of war. My grandfather would only talk in general terms and never detailed the horrors that he saw and suffered during those long years as a POW in Malaysian Peninsula. According to my mother he came back a changed man, physically and emotionally. He had always been a kind and caring person and in spite of the inhumanity he experienced during the war he became even more gentle and humane.

Abba Jee loved to shop, especially for food. Mangoes were his favourite fruit and he would go to the special wholesale fruit market to buy the best quality and variety of them. We ate the best mangoes the summers he spent with us. My earliest and one of my favourite memories of my grandfather is of him taking my cousin, my younger sister and me shopping to Qissa Khawani Bazaar in Peshawar for Eid when I was five years old. All four of us clipped-clopped to the market in a horse-drawn cab called 'Tonga'. Abba Jee bought each of us bangles and traditional white and gold embroidered shoes. Those bangles and slippers were preserved for posterity by my father in a black-and-white photograph.

Abba Jee was known for his honesty, fairness and kindness. Members of the family would seek his advice on family conflicts, knowing that he would have the most balanced view on the situation. Abba Jee lived his life on the principle that one should treat others as one would like to be treated. My siblings and I are blessed from having had the presence of this kind and gentle person in our lives. My hope is that we can pass the lessons learned from his life on to our children and grandchildren.

Aasia Mahmood was born in a small garrison town of Kohat. She spent her childhood in various military towns such as Peshawar, Quetta, Rawalpindi and Dhaka. She has been living in Scotland for the past 24 years, working as a bilingual support teacher and as an interpreter.

Sir John Major

When Harry, our grandson, lunched with the family the other day, he was asked where he wished to sit.

'Next to Granddad' he replied.

That was, for me, a moment of great pleasure.

There is only one joy in life equal to the love of a child, and that is the love of a grandchild. Harry and I are separated by nearly sixty years, yet each of us is able to learn something from the other. When we walk around the garden, with his small hand tucked into mine, I feel the warmth, trust and sheer innocence of youth. There is much cynicism in this world, but there is much more good. Each day I spend with my grandson, Harry, I am reminded of that.

The Rt Hon Sir John Major KG CH was Prime Minister of the United Kingdom from 1990 to 1997.

Terry Mansfield

By the time I was born, sadly both my grandfathers had passed away and my paternal grandmother lived more than fifty miles from us so I saw little of her because during the Second World War travel was not encouraged. My maternal grandmother had a big influence on my life and I remember clearly the Saturday morning ritual of black leading the grate, whitening the step, polishing the brass and my first responsibility – taking her accumulator to be recharged for her wireless and collecting the one from the week before! I hated my first glasses so much that I put them through her vast mangle and found myself in serious trouble!

My daughters, Anna and Victoria, were very fortunate in having my wife Helen's mother Margaret in their lives for a very long time and they saw her as being loving and fun. She devoted her life to their well-being and made it possible to always be available if we had to travel and she was the best babysitter in the world. We have the good fortune of having four grandchildren: Anna and her husband Adam's daughters are Clementine aged eleven, Eloise nine, and Victoria and Tim's children are Archie, seven and Kate, four.

When Archie was thirteen months he was struck down by a life-threatening brain virus and finished up in intense care at St George's Hospital, Tooting. They have an amazing paediatric unit that really did rescue him. My daughter Victoria wanted to repay the hospital staff and as a result created a bedtime story book compiled with the help of celebrities. *Stars at Bedtime* sold in excess of 100,000 copies and the outcome was it raised sufficient funds for the hospital to buy a desperately needed scanner. What was very extraordinary was a year to the day my granddaughter Eloise became seriously ill and finished up in the same ward but in the next bed. Therefore our grandchildren are particularly precious to us – so much so, that Helen my wife has become a trustee of a very worthwhile charity which is well worth joining – the Grandparents' Association. It is not generally realised that grandparents do not have rights of access and with so many families not staying together, this is a serious issue.

Terry Mansfield CBE retired as President and CEO of The National Magazine Company in 2004 and is now retained by The Hearst Corporation as Consultant. Amongst his many other activities he is Chairman of Graduate Fashion Week and works with both the London Week of Peace and the Historic Royal Palaces Campaign Board. Throughout his media career he has made it his mission to find the best talent in the industry.

Lady Doreen Massey

I am a fairly new grandparent. I could not have imagined how much joy and fun this would bring. I have again become immersed in buying children's books and toys with the happy thought that I could read to and play with Luke, aged six and Lara aged two (or, as she insists, two and a half).

When my husband and I stay with them, they love to crawl into bed with us in the morning for long relaxed cups of milk and lots of stories.

This experience of grandparenting contrasts with that of other grandparents who are the sole carers of their grandchildren. In my role of chair of a drugs organisation, I meet grandparents (usually grandmothers) who have taken on, out of love and necessity, the care of grandchildren because their own son or daughter has been imprisoned or has died from a drug overdose or is incapable of looking after children due to an addiction.

These grandparents need all the help and support they can get from social, health and education services, from friends and from organisations involved with grandparents. One such grandparent said, 'I feel lonely and unsupported. I am filling in forms for maintenance when I want to be reading stories to my grandson.'

Grandparenting should be full of enjoyment. I wish it were so for everyone.

Lady Doreen Massey is a former teacher and community playgroup organiser. She is now a Labour peer, speaking mainly on children and young people's issues. She is also a Lady Taverner, raising funds for disabled children to get involved in sport and Chair of the National Treatment Agency for Substance Misuse. She has three grown up children.

Nicola Mendelsohn

For obvious reasons you only know your grandparents when they are relatively old. And for some reason they never look as young as they should in old photographs of when they were young or newly married. It emphasises that they were of a different generation, that they were brought up in different times and that the world is a very different place.

Often the most we learn from grandparents is from how they moulded our parents into what they are. There are those – of whom I count myself one – who were fortunate enough to have been given a blueprint for life by the close contact I enjoyed with them for over thirty-five years.

Hilda Lily Patchinsky and Asher Chaim Sadofsky, or Grandma and Asher as I knew and adored them, had no qualifications and had already had tough lives by the time that they married.

They came from the generation that thought there were no short cuts to a good life. It required hard work, honesty, character and an unswerving commitment to their responsibilities as parents.

They had strong values. They always believed in getting on with it. Complaining or even stoicism just seemed like a waste of time. They were grateful for the little they had but knew through their endeavours each day they would be able to gain more in some way.

They were both from immigrant families. Asher's family came directly from Russia while Hilda's had detoured from the villages of Eastern Europe through Leeds and Belfast. Hilda had ended up in England when she and her siblings ran away to escape from a demonic stepmother.

Their aspirations were not about their own personal achievements but about their children. There was no sacrifice that they were not willing to make to ensure that they were given the opportunities that they never had.

They spent almost every hour of the day together. They did everything together and were a partnership of equals.

They were a permanent feature for twenty years at the haberdashery and fabric market stall they opened on the far corner of the upper floor of the Manchester Arndale Centre near to the Fountain Street entrance. They had graduated from the daily grind of touring the daily markets of the north-west, although my brothers and I will never forget the fun of the days before seat belts as we perched on top of the fabrics loaded up in the back of the van travelling to and from the Crewe Market – a particular favourite of Asher.

Their market stall was passed on in good shape but did not survive the IRA bomb that hit the city in 1996.

Asher was always interested in the world around him. He relied on the newspapers and the stories of others to provide his window on the world as he spent his time in a perpetual travelling circle around the UK.

Hilda couldn't stop working. They worked for many years after retirement and even after the 'hab and fab' sales she did a stint in curtain wear before starting a cottage bespoke greeting card service.

Hilda was diagnosed with cancer at forty-one. She beat it for another forty-one years until her body just couldn't withstand all the other shocks it suffered. Her iron will and determination to carry on kept her going through a litany of health problems. She never complained. Indeed, most of the time she withstood discomfort and pain without raising any concern at all. Later in life we started to see the signs of agony in the way she held herself or walked but she still steadfastly refused to acknowledge her ailments. Only just before she was finally felled by failing organs did she even talk about the suffering she endured for so long.

They both had the enormous pleasure to see their great-grandchildren come into the world and Hilda, who survived Asher by four years, was always lifted by every happy occasion and celebration that our family could generate.

There are many stories that represent their lives. But it is the example of how they lived their lives that will always keep their memories alive. They have set the benchmarks for my life.

Nicola Mendelsohn is Chair and partner of Karmarama. She is married to Jon and has four children, Gabi, Danny, Sam and Zac. She is also the Chair of the corporate board of Women's Aid, past President of Women in Advertising and Communications London, advisory board member of Cosmetic Executive Women and Director of the Fragrance Foundation.

Rhodri Morgan

I had a really strange experience last week – almost what you would call an 'out of body' experience. I actually heard my grandmother's voice for the first time in fifty-six years. She was chattering away about the family legend about a bit of folk medicine – a family heirloom called a snakestone, or Mamacal. My grandmother died in 1952!

So has the First Minister for Wales gone completely loopy and is now hearing voices among his many other sins? Have I become the Doris Stokes *de nos jours*, chinking upside-down tumblers around the dining table? No, it isn't like that actually, although that might make a more interesting story in some ways. But the story of how my grandmother came to make a tape recording in 1936, three years before I was born, and then how I heard it in 2008, is pretty weird. It means that my six grandchildren, aged between eight and two, have all now heard thier great-great-grandmother's voice talking as though she was still here, when in fact she died half a century before they were born.

She recorded her story about the snakestone because she spoke an industrial-area dialect of Welsh from the Llansamlet area of Swansea – then the heartlands of the zinc and copper smelting industry. The kind of Welsh she spoke, with industrial inflections and peculiarities, was suspected not to be able to survive the impact of the Great Depression and the forces of Anglicisation as they travelled along the A48 east-west artery of transport which passed right through Llansamlet on the way from London to Cardiff and all points east on its way to Swansea and westward to Carmarthen and Pembrokeshire. My grandmother was an endangered species, in other words!

It is wonderful to hear my grandmother's voice again when she meant so much to me because she died in our house in 1952 and I in turn had nearly died in her house in 1942 when I was three years old and contracted pneumonia during a Christmas holiday. It must have been pretty awful for grandparents and parents if one of your children got pneumonia in those days before antibiotics. All you could do was to keep a coal fire in the bedroom and have the GP on hand and if the temperature went up and over 103, or whatever it is, that was the end of you.

I survived. Sadly, my grandmother did not survive cancer of the womb, which she developed in 1949. I remember to this day the terrors of the somewhat primitive radium therapy treatment that was all that was available sixty years ago. I recall my mother telling me what the consultant had told my grandmother to warn he of the painful side effects of undergoing radium therapy in those days. The consultant had said, 'Mrs Rees, it's going to be very painful.'

My grandmother asked, 'Well, how painful?'

And the doctor replied, 'Do you remember child-birth? And on getting a nod from my grandmother, he said, 'Well, it's going to be a thousand times more painful than that, but your heart is as strong as a horse, so you should be able to survive it'!

I think that particular consultant may have just been brutally honest or he had missed out the 'bedside manner' module at medical school.

When the treatment failed, or rather the cancer came back a second time, she couldn't have another dose of radium therapy. Only morphine and trying to control the pain was left. It used to be my job to run down to the chemist to sign the Poisons Register and pick up my grandmother's morphine. I'd then usually nip in the newsagent next door to the chemist to buy the *Dandy* or the *Beano* and walk back with my oddly assorted shopping basket of morphine and comics. I don't think Health and Safety regulations would allow that now. My grandmother was probably, to all intense and purposes, an opium addict by the time she died and I suppose I was the unwitting agent of that but it saved her the terrible pain of her cancer.

The other legend about my grandmother is that she had been warned by her prospective mother-in-law on no account to marry my grandfather, John Rees, because he was far too stubborn ever to be a decent husband to anyone! Perhaps that is where my stubborn streak comes from. Luckily for me, my grandmother ignored the advice.

By an odd coincidence my mother had introduced my father as a prospective husband to my grandfather and grandmother and he had his tea and cakes and left. My mother asked my grandparents, 'what do you think of him?' My stubborn 'man of few words' grandfather grunted '*siarad gormod*' – which means 'He talks too much' – so there's another genetic cross I bear!

The actual legend that she talks about on the tape recording made in 1936 was about a snakestone; in Llansamlet dialect Welsh – a 'Mamacal' – a prized family heirloom which we still own. A snakestone is formed by a congregation of young male adders fighting for supremacy and leaving behind the kind of congealed amalgam of spit, venom and goo which then forms a ring-shaped residue, supposed to have magic powers to cure sties or other eye ailments.

It could either be applied direct on the eye or more usually used to form a potion by pouring boiling water over the stone and waiting for the water to cool to a temperature when it could be used as an eye lotion.

It was part of a small business-dominated Welsh society where if you could make a halfpenny or a penny from hiring out the snakestone, it was a valuable top-up to the family income.

This was not the National Health Service, after all.

Not only does it pre-date the National Health

Service, it may even go back to druidic times, according to accounts written by Pliny describing this kind of folk medicine in use in Roman Gaul as well as Celtic Britain.

I imagine that at least one member of the Royal Family might feel deeply comforted that the First Minister for Wales still keeps a prized family heirloom, a homeopathic treatment for eye ailments going back to the druids!

As one of my cousins had been one of Wales' leading ophthalmologists over the past thirty years until she recently retired, I am not sure what she would think of this legend, although certainly she was very fond of my grandmother too.

Hearing my grandmother's voice and seeing the wonderment of my own grandchildren listening to their great-great-grandmother's voice is really a very special experience and reminds us of how the generations are all bound together. I just happen to be one of the lucky ones that can bring together five generations of one family via the tricks of the trade of the early tape recorders and the later generation's CDs to hear that mellifluous voice and that wonderful Llansamlet dialect and that weird Celtic legend of the magic snakestone that cured people's eye infection before the NHS and modern spectacles broke the link with our ancient past.

Rhodri Morgan became First Minister for Wales in 2000. He is married to Julie Morgan, MP for Cardiff North. They have three children and seven grandchildren.

In the Company of My Grandpa

Callum Munro

When I was at school I was asked to write an essay about an individual of importance in my life. I wrote about my grandfather, and I read an extract at his funeral.

For as long as I can remember, the only male to figure constantly in my life has been my grandfather. He was there when I was born and has been there ever since. As you can imagine, the nature of this relationship may therefore differ slightly from that which exists between an average grandfather and grandson. Yet in terms of male figures in my life, I feel in no way that I lack something or someone, but that I am privileged. I have many friends who have never formed close relationships with their grandparents, and I feel sorry for these people – my friends and their grandparents – as I believe strongly in the role that a relationship like mine can play in an individual's life, regardless of his or her parental situation.

When I was four, I moved with my mother to Edinburgh to live with my grandparents. This is where I feel my childhood truly began. It was in the bedroom that I chose on the top floor of my grandparents' house that I would live for the next five years of my life. It is this house that springs immediately to mind at any mention of the notion of 'home' and provides the setting for some of my fondest and most nostalgic memories, especially those involving my grandfather.

One of my most vivid memories is of my grandpa walking me to school on my very first day. Walking hand in hand, I let my grandfather understand in no un-certain terms how I felt about where we were going. Whenever we walked past a lamppost on impulse I reached out with my free left hand and clung to the dog-pee covered, metallic saviour for dear life. Having had one of his two (myopic) eyes on me the entire time my grandpa anticipated my desperate actions with little difficulty. Yet, never one to display bad humour, he walked a few paces forward until the chain of linked arms and lamppost felt the strain. At this point, much to my surprise, he let out a hefty bellow of fake befuddle-ment and stumbled back as if to fall, but strangely was able to just catch himself before doing so. The degree of hilarity with which I greeted this is nearly impossible to describe. After all, I would have to walk to school every day and both my grandpa and I, with undoubtedly dissimilar feelings on the matter, realised exactly what this would entail.

It is these ever-present displays of energy, spontaneity and genuine interest in the well-being of his grandchildren and children – even with the inevitable onset of old age – that I believe makes my grandfather special. It is easy to imagine another grandparent in a similar situation to that which I have described showing an utter lack of patience for the annoying young kid I was. (Although my grandpa was of course no angel; I could write as much again about tales of youthful escapades in his company.)

Like every relationship ours has undergone changes, but what stands out most is my overriding belief in, and respect for my grandfather. As a child I sincerely believed my grandpa was the funniest man in the world. When I grew older and moved away to St Andrews, we did not grow apart as might be expected but were drawn closer together as the distance between us made our meetings that bit more unusual and enjoyable. As I reflect on the five-or-so years between then and now I find it incredible to list in my head the many amazing opportunities my grandparents' generosity has brought my way. It is a lucky person whose grandparents have taken the trouble to show their grandchild many, diverse, regions of the world.

Today I see my grandfather as my ultimate role model. To have grown up impoverished as he did, and then to have studied at university and had a renowned professional career, to be married for forty-three years, and to still have a more hectic social life at sixty-seven than I do at sixteen, is quite an achievement. I feel that he has influenced me in so many ways, from supporting his football team and sharing his sense of humour, to developing my sense of moral judgement. His liberal attitudes and political beliefs have never been forced upon me but I cannot help feeling compelled to share them. When I look at my grandfather today, I am filled with admiration and a feeling of the utmost respect. I like to believe that our relationship has evolved since I was a child to become a friendship between adults.

Kenneth Munro was born in very humble circumstances in Glasgow on 17th December 1936 and was educated at Glasgow University, where he became a socialist and supporter of the European movement. Latterly he was the Head of the EU representation in Scotland. He loved Scotland and he loved people – and a great many people from all walks of life loved him.

Callum Munro is currently studying at Glasgow University, but wrote this piece as a high school essay. He delivered a version of it at his Grandfather's funeral in St Giles Cathedral in Edinburgh in 2008.

Granfeddy – Ice cream floats and Morse code

Carol Murray

My granddad, or Granfeddy as I called him, died in 1978 when I was just eleven years old. Two things about him always come to mind: ice cream floats and Morse code.

Most days of the school summer holidays Granfeddy would come over to my house and we would walk to the small café nearby and he would buy me an ice cream float, usually coke with a huge dollop of vanilla ice cream.

Rainy afternoons were usually spent sending Morse code messages. Granfeddy would leave messages and I would have to find them then decode them. The messages always revealed the whereabouts of bags of toffees and other treats that Granfeddy had hidden, usually under the bed or the big kitchen dresser. It wasn't till a few years after his death I asked myself why all the Morse code? It turned out that Granfeddy had been a signaller in the Black Watch during the First World War.

Carol Murray is a Community Midwife at Forth Park Hospital in Kirkcaldy Fife as well as being the Granny School coordinator – a project funded by PiggyBankKids.

Baroness Julia Neuberger

My grandmother, Anna Schwab, was a very remarkable woman. Born in Frankfurt, in Germany, her father died when she was very young and she went out to work to support her family. She eventually left Germany to marry my grandfather, a banker in London, and never did paid work again. She spent the rest of her life in London, had three sons, and never stopped working until frailty hit her in her seventies.

As a volunteer, she ran children's nurseries in the East End of London, ran girls' clubs for poor young women, to give them somewhere to go in the evening and a place they could acquire new skills. She helped with baby clinics long before the NHS was invented – all run by volunteers, providing orange juice for poor families and making sure the toddlers developed normally. Later, she was a passionate campaigner to bring Jewish refugees to England during the Nazi years, as well as the chair of the Welfare Committee of the Refugee Committee, looking after those who reached England and finding accommodation and work for them. Those years of desperation for German Jews were the years when she worked hardest, tirelessly, trying to make a difference – and she succeeded. By the time I knew her, she was already physically frail and mainly stayed at home. But her spirit was indomitable and her mind as quick as ever. And she was a wonderful grandmother.

I used to go and see her after school a couple of times a week. Patiently, she would listen to me doing my music theory – or, even worse for her, she would listen to me practise the violin – I was never any good. She would argue, discuss and support my decisions and this when I was very young – she died when I was thirteen.

Among so many other stories I could tell about her, my favourite memory of this very remarkable woman is from when I was six. My parents were really very short of money, and all my clothes were hand-me-downs from my cousins. In 1956, my grandmother decided she would buy all her granddaughters new dresses for Passover. It was a relatively rare outing to go anywhere with her, and we went packed into two taxis – unbelievable luxury – to a children's clothes shop on Finchley Road. I can still see the shop in my mind's eye now, and smell that scent I still love of brand-new fabrics and plush coat-hangers. It was the period where stiff net petticoats were, for six-year-olds, the acme of high fashion, the absolute winner at every children's party. She bought me my dream dress, even though my aunt Anne, who was with us for this expedition, kept saying how unsuitable it was – and it was.

The dress gave my mother nightmares – stiff, frilly, with dozens of pale blue net petticoats, it had the further disadvantage of needing to be dry-cleaned. As I always spilled stuff on my clothes, my mother could see mounting bills from each wearing of this glorious garment. But I loved it. And my grandmother, when my aunt remonstrated with her about unpractical it was, just kept saying that the child should have what she wanted. She had decided to buy us all dresses and we were to choose them. If that is what I wanted, that is what I should have. And have it I did – pale blue silk, stiff net petticoats embroidered all over – very, very satisfactory. I loved that dress. But, more than that, I loved that grandmother who, knowing it was ridiculous, allowed me, as a small child, to indulge my whims and my ghastly taste. I still think she was right. And how I loved her for letting me do it.

Baroness Julia Neuberger is a rabbi, a Liberal Democrat member of the House of Lords, an author, and a passionate campaigner for older people, asylum seekers, volunteers and volunteering.

Phil Neville

I have been extremely fortunate in that I had all of my grandparents up until two years ago, therefore I have many, many fond memories of them and they have been a big part of my life.

One thing that does make me smile about not just my grandparents but elderly people in general is how they always speak their minds and speak the truth – often at inappropriate times!

There was never any chance of me getting carried away with my footballing success, in particular with my granddad Alec. When coming off the pitch after a match the first things he would say to me was 'You were bloody rubbish.' At the time I though these were harsh words but on looking back, it was his way of keeping me grounded and striving to be better.

If I had to sum up in a short space what I remember most about my grandparents – it has to be that they were always the people who would let us have the things or do the things our parents said 'no' to: crisps, chocolates, television, late nights!

I feel blessed to have had such wonderful grandparents and am indebted to them for everything they ever gave me, taught me and the time they spent with me.

Phil Neville is a professional footballer who played for Manchester United until 2005 when he transferred to Everton, where he became captain. He also plays for the England team.

Tracy-Ann Oberman

My grandma Lilly was the world to me when I was very little. Sadly she was only in my life till I was five years old but she had such a profound effect on me. She was larger than life and always smelled beautiful and dressed immaculately and wouldn't be seen dead outside the house without hat, coat and gloves. She was a true lady and everything that surrounded her was beautiful and elegant and a little European. She also made me feel special and loved and adored.

My other grandma, Grandma Fay, was around for a lot longer in my life although sadly not now for over fifteen years. She was a homemaker, always in a pinny, frying fish, or making fairy cakes, peeling a pear for my sister and me, or boiling up the world's truly best chicken soup. She had a little red docile dachshund called Whiskey.

I remember having sleepovers in my mum's old bedroom and then having a delicious breakfast of fresh hot white toast (perched in a rack) and honey and then during the summer holidays spending hours with my sister Debra running in and out of the sprinkler in the garden in our knickers and vests.

Grandma Fay may have been a homemaker but she also had a killer sense of humour, an eye for a bargain, and an innate sense of the stockmarket. When she died it turned out she had a keen portfolio that no one knew about.

Both sets of grandmothers were survivors, from pogroms, the slums of the East End, fathers lost in the Great War, cousins and loved ones obliterated in the concentration camps of Europe. These young girls dragged themselves up from nothing, helping their new husbands form market stalls to later opening clothes shops ('The first in the East End to sell jeans,' Fay would boast proudly). They ran their homes and families with military precision, making sure that their children had everything that they had not.

I admire them now more than I can say and I wish that I could have the chance to meet both my grandmas now just for an hour to honour them, to ask questions and talk woman to woman, mother to mother. Their wisdom would come in useful. Grandmas serve a huge familial purpose.

Now I am a mother I see my own mother in a totally different light. She is a wonderful grandmother: patient (far more now than when I was little), adoring, kind, and entranced with my little girl. Anoushka, for her part, sees the light of the world in her grandma Issy. Sadly no grandpas for my little Anoushka but Grandma Issy more than makes up as her role of matriach to our little family with her endless time, cookery lessons (I only peeled the plastic off the cooker the day I bought my baby home from the hospital), love and patience and advice. She carries on the grand family tradition of strong, memorable, warm, embracing, intelligent grandmothers who live long in the heart.

Tracy-Ann Oberman is a well known theatre, TV and radio actress, most recognisable for her portrayal of Chrissie Watts in Eastenders *and Yvonne Hartman in* Dr Who. *As a writer she originated and co-authored 3* Sisters on Hope Street *for the Hampstead Theatre, winning the BBC2 Greenlight Award. She has been a columnist for the* Guardian *and the* JC.

Julia Ogilvy

Although my maternal grandparents died some years ago I still feel their influence. I often think of the simpler life they led, running a fruit farm in East Anglia, holidaying on the nearby coast and making family the focus of their lives.

I will always remember the joy my grandfather felt when he came to stay with us in Scotland and was able to hold his great-grandchildren in his arms. He was immensely proud of my business career but always wanted me to take things easier and look after myself better.

My grandmother's funeral was a turning point in my life as people recalled her role as a beloved mother, grandmother and friend. I realised how unimportant business success would be in comparison to this and vowed to make more time for family and friends in my life.

Julia Ogilvy is founder and chairman of Project Scotland, a national volunteering organisation for young Scots. She won many awards in her business career as MD of Hamilton and Inches, including Scottish Businesswoman of the Year and recently the Scottish Social Entrepreneur of the Year Award.

Imogen Parker

When I was a little girl, my gran used to tell me a story called 'The Magic Teapot'. It was about a child who invited her friends to a birthday party, but instead of buying food and drink, her mother spent their last few pennies on a rusty old teapot she spotted in the window of an antique shop. The little girl was very sad with nothing except tea to offer her guests, but, miraculously, the teapot poured whatever drink they wished for – raspberry milkshake, strawberry cordial, pineapple fizz!

The story resonated with elements of my own life – my family lived too far away from my primary school for me to ever invite my friends over; my father had once had a junk shop, and our house was cluttered with rusty, dented old artifacts nobody wanted; the most exotic drink I had ever encountered was orange squash – but I'm sure my gran didn't design consciously for me, she was just a natural storyteller. With grown-up eyes, I can see that 'The Magic Teapot' owed a lot to the story of Aladdin and the recently released film of *Mary Poppins*; as a child, I thought it was brilliantly original, and demanded to hear it again and again.

My gran was born at the end of the nineteenth century when Queen Victoria was still on the throne, and the stories she used to tell about her childhood were as intriguing as the fictions she made up. As a little girl, she would stand on a stool in the kitchen pretending to be one of the suffragettes she had seen speaking on the street corner, and her mother would laugh until tears ran down her face.

My gran was a true cockney, born within the sound of Bow bells, but her parents were immigrants from Germany and in the First World War, a mob came to their shop and smashed it up, and my gran was lifted over the back wall with a bag of sovereigns from the safe and told to run and tell the police. After that, the family never spoke German and brought their children up in ignorance of their origins. At the beginning of the Second World War, with a young family of her own, my gran was so frightened the mob would come again, she ruined the lunch she was cooking and forgot to put salt in the potatoes.

It wasn't an easy life, working six days a week from the age of fourteen at the chilly counter of a butcher's shop, bringing up three children through the war years, and married to a bad-tempered, jealous man. Sometimes my gran's stories had a darker edge – cautionary tales, perhaps – but the underlying theme was always a determination to make the best of things. Her reward was to retire to a very modest, semi-detached house in the suburbs. Having spent her whole life in inner-city London without so much as a windowbox, my gran discovered that she was as natural a gardener as she was a storyteller, turning a narrow strip of lawn into a paradise of flowering shrubs she cultivated from cuttings, with a peach tree, bearing luscious ripe peaches, that she grew from a stone.

Like the teapot in my favourite story, my gran had the magical gift of making ordinary things wonderful. When I visited as a child, she helped me sew dolls' clothes from scraps of crushed crepe with a floral print that had once been her best dress, and baked marble cake, every slice revealing a different swirly pattern of chocolate and plain sponge. Sometimes, I was allowed into the cold front room to wind up the gramophone and, with the door closed so my grandfather's afternoon nap wouldn't be disturbed, we would listen to a crackling crooner singing 'The Isle of Capri', and my gran's eyes would glaze with the impossible romance of the lyrics.

She was such a sunny, attractive person that even though she was well into her sixties, she received three proposals of marriage in the year after my grandfather died, but she chose to remain on her own, enjoying her independence, and bought a second-hand piano, which she taught herself to play even though her hands were stiff with arthritis.

When I visited her as a grown up, we'd sit in her lovely garden with cups of tea, and she'd demand to hear tales of my university life – parties, travels, lovers and dreams – delighting in all the new fashions and freedoms, and laughing until tears ran down her face.

Imogen Parker's recent trilogy of novels, The Time of Our Lives, The Things We Do For Love *and* This Little World, *is a fictional history of post-war Britain.*

Charlie Parsons

My father's mother died when I was seven, in her late eighties, so I hardly knew her. She was from another generation with different values and a different outlook. Her many grandchildren, including myself, were inspired with a family story of how she proved faith and conviction could move mountains and showed how nothing should be accepted at face value.

In 1928, when my uncle, then aged seventeen, was paralysed in a rugby accident at school, she called in London's most respected orthopedic surgeon, a man with many titles and who had treated royalty. He told her: 'I have bad news for you, your son will be dead within a week.'

She said, 'What is your fee? I will write you a cheque but do not cash it yet as I do not believe you.'

He said, 'What are you going to do?'

My grandmother replied, 'I am going to take him home and nurse him.'

The famous man said, 'You are a murderer, Mrs Parsons.'

'Well,' she said, 'a murderer I will be.'

Later in her life, the doctor came and apologized, saying it was the only time in his life he had been wrong in assessing what care and conviction could do.

My uncle did die eventually but he lived for more than a year even though he couldn't move or feed himself. But all of her grandchildren have taken away the lesson that strength and conviction is more important than titles, fame and so called expertise.

Charlie Parsons has won many awards for creating groundbreaking television programmes, including two Emmys for Survivor, *the first reality show on television, which 10 years after it began is still on CBS in America. In the UK, he was responsible for* The Word *and the* Big Breakfast. *He is also a journalist and theatre producer.*

Angad Paul

As a child, I was only able to know one of my grandparents. As much as my time with her was wonderful, I see ever more clearly through my nieces, nephews and now my own children the how special the relationship is.

The instant recognition and connection between children and their grandparents is something that gives true meaning to life. There is a level of unconditional love and compassion that is unique and flows both ways, obeying forces that only become more relevant as children grow older in what can be troubling world.

Just to see the interaction between my children and their grandparents is to understand happiness (and sometimes, as a parent, jealousy). Children will always love their parents, but they can do no wrong in the eyes of their grandparents!

Now I truly know that my grandmother, Naniji (as I knew her), is strong in spirit and watching over me always.

The Hon. Angad Paul is Chief Executive of Caparo plc. Aside from his business interests he is Patron of the SHINE Education Trust and the youngest Trustee of Slough Grammar School.

Lord Paul

I'm lucky enough to have eight grandchildren – three boys and three girls aged between eighteen and twenty-three – then another girl aged three years old and a one-year-old boy. So there is almost a generation between the first set of grandchildren and the second.

There are not many people who are given the opportunity to have two generations of grandchildren. There is no doubt that I love them all equally, but my wife and I have been able to really enjoy the childhood of the second set as we are of an age to be able to spend so much more time with them.

Our children were born when I was in my late twenties and thirties – the part of my life when I was working hardest to establish my career – and fighting with myself to be able to spend time with them.

The first six grandchildren came along when we were in our fifties and still working hard. I had some time to spare, but never as much as I would have liked. I greatly enjoyed my time with them while they were growing up, but I can't help but feel that it wasn't quite enough. When the three elder boys were aged around ten, we took them on a tour of Europe and then did the same for the three girls. Then we took all of them on a cruise when they were in their teens. They were certainly the most enjoyable holidays we have had. Now that they are older, I treasure the excellent relationship that both myself and my wife have with them as they make their own way in the world.

Our two youngest grandchildren were born when we were in to our seventies and finally had more time to spend with the family. I for one, until the arrival of my three-year-old granddaughter, had never given a child a bottle. I could not have imagined that the experience of feeding my grandchild could bring so much joy. We are involved in their daily lives and I would not have it any other way.

For those of you who have grown-up children with no offspring, tell them to get to work quick! I can highly recommend being a grandparent to anyone.

Lord (Swraj) Paul of Marylebone is a leading businessman who was born in India and came to the UK in the 1960s and founded the Caparo Group. He was awarded the Padma Bhushan by the Government of India in 1983. Made a peer in 1996, he became a deputy speaker of the House of Lords in 2008. As well as being Chairman of the Board and Trustee of PiggyBankKids, he also set up the Ambika Paul Foundation which supports children and education.

Shyama Perera

When I was four, I spent several months living in the home of my maternal grandparents in Sri Lanka. My memories of that time, however, do not really feature them. I remember suffering badly from prickly heat and yowling as servants covered my body in freshly boiled leaves that were supposed to alleviate the symptoms.

I remember the well in their park-sized garden, and the huge iguanas that lumbered through. At the front were jackfruit trees, sugar cane that would be cut down and given to me to chew, and a pale yellow Morris Minor parked away from the verandah. At some point during my stay, my father joined us and devil dancers were called to perform a ceremony on him. Were they happy days? I honestly couldn't tell you.

My paternal grandparents, Alice and Alexander Perera, were already dead when my parents married. In the family album there is a faded sepia photograph of them with their children: Noel, Oliver, Irene and Gregory. I rarely look at it and, because my parents separated in England a few months after that devil dance of distant memory, I know nothing about them.

My mother's parents, Don Charles and Dona Milina Wijesinghe, had spent all their lives in the southern hamlet of Getamana. I know they were caring and dutiful towards their five daughters and their twelve other grandchildren, but the huge distances between us meant I had no sense of engagement with them. I saw them only once after settling in London. I was eighteen and on a three-week visit. They were small, sweet and indescribably foreign. They cried when they saw me and I stood, smiling but embarrassed, feeling self-conscious and awkward under their inspection. It is only now, seeing how much my own children benefit from their extremely close relationship with my mother, and regular and lively contact with their father's parents, that I realise what I might have had – and what I might have learned.

The most important lesson, beyond the safe place offered by grandparents; beyond the kindness, the love, the time and the treats given; is a respect and affection for older members of society. I grew up with only my mother for adult company; as a result I regarded anyone older as an authority figure to be either challenged or, later, going through school, obeyed and feared. My daughters see them as better-informed, interesting and helpful companions on the road that they themselves travel. They are appreciative, deferential and interested in what all elders – myself included – have to offer; in other words, they have grown to be better-rounded, kinder and more socially competent members of the community.

To me, then, the contribution of a grandparent is not limited to the well-being of the child, or to babysitting or making fancy dress outfits or sponsoring their grandchildren in races and tasks, it is about preparing the young to take on the world, which means understanding their part in a society where every right-thinking individual plays, and continues to play a part, right to the end.

Shyama Perera is a novelist, journalist and columnist.

My Irish Grandmother
Gervase Phinn

Grandma Mullarkey was a striking-looking woman. She had clear penetrating blue eyes, high arching brows, long dark eyelashes, thick lustrous silver hair, fine hands and a sensuous oval face. Of medium height, she was neither thickset nor thin and until age crept up on her she held her body stiffly upright. Like many of Irish stock, she possessed that Celtic combination of levity and seriousness. Laughter and tears were never far apart. She was a fine storyteller, a keen and discerning reader and an avid letter writer. The correspondence with her relations in Ireland, some of which survives to this day, displays her gift with words and strong command of the language. The letters are written in the most beautifully formed copperplate handwriting; the grammar is exact and there isn't a spelling mistake to be seen.

My grandmother was a devout Roman Catholic and a great believer in the power of prayer and, until the time came when she became infirm and house bound, a regular attendee at confession and mass. Hers, however, was a questioning faith and she would not be afraid of tackling the priest about certain edicts of the Church, which was unusual and brave in an age when the priest's word was law and to question it was close to sacrilege.

On one occasion, I must have been about fifteen at the time, I entered into a discussion with her about heaven and hell. As a Catholic, I was taught quite unequivocally what happened after death and where I would end up. If I lived a blameless life and repented of all my sins, I would end up in heaven. If I didn't and had done something really bad, I would be condemned to the flames of hell for all time. There was the other place: limbo. This was the abode of the souls of unbaptised infants and of the just who died before Christ. Those in limbo suffered no pain or consciousness but would never see the face of God. It seemed to me, a questioning adolescent, that this arrangement was rather unfair and not in keeping with a benevolent God. Surely He would not consign these innocents who – through no fault of their own – had died unbaptised or unfortunately had lived before the coming of Jesus to such a cold and empty place. My grandmother listened to what I had to say and effectively ended any discussion with the words, 'Limbo. Stuff and nonsense.' I was pleased to learn some years later that the Catholic Church came around to her way of thinking.

Grandma's use of English would have fascinated the connoisseur of the colloquial; she had a rich variety of speech often possessed by the Irish – lively, colourful, vibrant – and shared with her three daughters an acerbic turn of phrase when speaking of those she disliked. Her comments on the failings and the unfortunate appearances of others were never mordacious or malicious because in their humour there was a sort of warmth and the listener could not help but smile. Her idioms were legendary in the family:

'She's that good, she bites the altar rails.'

'He has eyes like a couple of cold, fried eggs.'

'She has a mouth like a torn pocket.'

'He's as much use a grave robber in a crematorium.'

'If she died with that face on her, nobody would wash the corpse.'

'It runs in the family like Kitty O'Hara's nose.'

'A shut mouth catches no flies.'

'He's so fond of work, he'd lie down beside it.'

'She has an expression like last year's rhubarb.'

'If he was thrown after you, you wouldn't turn around to see what the clatter was.'

I once took a friend to see her, a boy with red hair and very prominent front teeth. 'Poor lad,' commiserated my grandmother, 'that young fellow could eat a tomato through a tennis racket.' On another occasion, on seeing a particularly fractious and unfortunate-looking pair of twins creating havoc on a bus she was said to have remarked: 'The mother, poor woman, would have been better off with a pair of jugs.'

Her son-in-law, my uncle Ted, sometimes unfairly I have to say, came in for his share of criticism and when Grandma wanted to divulge something to my mother that she didn't want Ted to hear, she would close the door. 'I don't want old loppy lugs listening,' she would say. 'That man comes into the room as quiet as a drop of soot.' Deep down of course she had a strong affection for her son-in-law and as she grew older and more infirm her comments about Uncle Ted were more approving.

I looked forward to the Sunday visits because Grandma Mullarkey took a particular interest in my reading and writing. I cannot pinpoint the precise moment when I came to the decision that I wanted to be a writer but certainly on those occasions when I sat with my grandmother listening to her stories and anecdotes, her reminiscences and commentaries, the seed was sown.

As a child I would take along with me on my visits the book of the moment: *Kidnapped* or *White Fang*, *Moonfleet* or *Children of the New Forest*, and we would read quietly together. At other times she would read to me from one of the large illustrated books she kept in a shelf near her bed. One favourite was *Swiss Family Robinson* with its garish coloured plates and big print. I loved the story where all the members of the shipwrecked family work happily together under the benign guidance of a father who was both strong and wise and who sported bulging muscles and a long chestnut beard.

When my grandma read, I thrilled at the sound of the words, the rhythms and the rhymes and would sit goggle-eyed at the power of her voice and her extraordinary memory. She knew passages of verse by heart and had a natural feel for measure and stress. I still recall snippets of verse she would recite:

And down the long and silent street
The dawn, with silver sandalled feet,
Creeps like a frightened girl.

I learned later these were lines written by Oscar Wilde, one of her favourite writers. She might not, I guess, have approved of his personal life but she loved his poems and stories as I do.

It was my Grandma Mullarkey who bought me my first dictionary when I started secondary school and the treasured portable Olivetti typewriter with the black and red ribbon so I could practise at being a writer. She would sit and listen as I read my early efforts while my mother would be in the kitchen talking to Aunt Nora. Sometimes she would nod in the manner of a dowager and make a small noise of satisfaction but at other times there would be a slight raise of the eyebrow, a brief lift of the chin, a small shake of the head and she would tell me gently the story or the poem could be improved. I learned about plot, character, style and other textbook concepts well before I came across them later in my schooling. I was never undeterred by my grandmother's comments, disappointed but never deflated. I learned a lesson for all would-be writers: if you cannot accept constructive criticism and if you are unwilling to persevere with your work then give it up.

Grandma, interested in world events, politics and religion, was also fascinated by people and taught me another invaluable lesson for the would-be writer: to be curious and observant. 'If you don't understand something,' she would say, 'then ask somebody and if they can't tell you, then go to the library and get a book.'

I was encouraged by my grandma to question, watch, listen, seek out and as a consequence I became a curious child, eager to know things. From an early age I became adept at observation. I would never intrude in a conversation but would like to observe, and eavesdrop: I would steal, glean, collect information and anecdote and always felt that in some strange way, I was storing these impressions for some future date. To this day I still love to watch people and to listen to them. I will sit behind a couple of elderly women on the bus, overhear a snippet of conversation in the doctor's waiting room, discreetly observe the angry customer berating a poor shop assistant, and store them at the back of my mind for possible future use. I can't do anything about it; after so many years, I am programmed to do it.

Grandma Mullarkey opened a door in my early childhood and changed my life for the better and when she died she left a great a gap. When I was sixteen I accompanied my mother to Doncaster Gate Hospital in Rotherham where my grandmother was dying of stomach cancer. There is no image in my childhood that I carry with me more clearly than the one of my grandmother in the hospital bed. She looked pale and weary propped up in the bed clutching her rosary beads, but her eyes were as bright and intelligent as ever. She told me not to look so miserable. 'Remember, she said, 'a smile will gain you ten years of life.'

She died the following day, clutching her rosary beads.

Dr Gervase Phinn leads a very full and busy life: he is a teacher, professor, freelance lecturer, author, poet and educational consultant. He is married with four grown up children.

Ruth Rendell

Scandinavian children call their maternal grandparents Mormor and Morfar and their paternal grandparents Farmor and Farfar. It is a neat and simple system and avoids confusion when you are referring to your fore-bears. My mother was a Dane brought up in Sweden and with a Swedish passport, so doubly Scandivanian, and to me her parents were Mormor and Morfar.

They lived in Stockholm, then in Copenhagen and came to London in 1905. Morfar who was a painter, carpenter and inventor and mad about cars, made a lot of money selling cars, lost it again and then made a bit more. By the time he was my grandfather, he was an elegant old man with white hair and beard who possessed two cars of his own, an ancient box-shaped Fiat and an even larger Opel, in one of which he used to visit us on Sunday after-noons to talk to my father about all the people who were swindling him out of what little money he had left. One of these, by chance, lived in a house visible from our windows. Morfar would shake his fist in the direction of this house, uttering imprecations in his execrable English: 'He schwinded me!' He boasted of being trilingual in

Danish, German and English and he may have been but I suspect he was coherent only in Danish.

Slender, beautiful and humourless, Mormor expected deference from all, especially her children and grandchildren. She used to say that Morfar had only married her for her dowry, pitifully small though it was, something I doubted as fifty years later she was still extremely good-looking. She ruled him with a rod of iron, literally with a rod with which she poked him when she wanted him to fetch something for her. I remember her mainly from her smothering yet somehow unfeeling hugs and her refusal ever to let me play her piano, while my other grandmother would have let me play hers all day long.

Ruth Rendell is a crime novelist who also writes as Barbara Vine. Many of her books have been adapted for film and television. She is a Fellow of the Royal Society of Literature, was awarded the CBE in 1996 and has been a Life Peer for twelve years.

David Robinson

When my big brother was learning to speak before I was born he inexplicably pronounced Granddad as Wogga. Even more improbably the name stuck and I never knew my paternal grandfather by any other name.

Wogga was fun. We played games endlessly when he visited. Often boisterous, competitive games that he always tried to win, cheating if necessary. If the foul play was discovered he would wink with a huge grin like he never meant it anyway but I always knew he did because I did too. We boxed with him, never with anybody else, and played football and rugby with little regard for the rules or, I now realise, my granddad's increasingly fraility. He recognised no weaknesses, worrying my father constantly with vigorous contempt for his own and others' safety.

At Christmas we traditionally played the balloon game. The object was simple – two teams faced one another from two lines of chairs, each attempting to bash the balloon over the heads of the opposing team. It was a lawless ritual without my Granddad. With him it was wild and dangerous and almost unbearably exciting. Then one year he reached back with such sudden violence that the sofa and its contents – him, my mother and me – toppled over backwards. The sofa was broken. His septuagenarian back must have sustained some damage too, though he never said. Words were spoken with my father and the game was never played again.

He was mischievous, irreverent and kind; with us children more child than adult, a compulsive storyteller, an enthusiast for everything and a bundle of energy. He swore, never in anger, but often to colour the tale. We loved him for it all but we knew that deeper down there was darkness.

Wogga had lied about his age to join Kitchener's first 100,000. It was a lie I never fully fathomed. Perhaps if I had experienced a harsh working-class childhood in bleak Edwardian London I would have understood it better. All my memories of my days with him are peppered by his memories of the war. It was never far from any conversation. Thrilling at the risqué humour and the raw excitement in my younger years, understanding more as I grew older. At the age when I was listening to the radio and dozing at the back in Fifth Form physics he was 'watching the fireworks' with eyes that seldom shut through long days and endless nights shin deep in mud and giant rats and dead men's boots. No wonder he could still see it all, bold as day, day in day out. At the going down of the sun and in the morning he was still there, sixty years on.

He was one of the few that survived the Western front from its innocent beginnings throughout its savage turmoil to its final feeble exhaustion four years later. He was back before his twenty-first birthday. It broke men and it changed them. I often wondered who he would have been if he hadn't been there in those fragile, formative years. I think it made him tough, fiercely independent, intensely strong-willed and just a little too guarded if you ever tried to go too deep. He rarely spoke of the suffering and only then when coaxed out of him, visiting as an adult, just the two of us in his tiny kitchen. The rest was jollity, the pranks, the camaraderie, the larger-than-life characters, often larger even than they were the last time we heard the story.

It wasn't until after he died that my cousin, working through regimental records told us how he had won the Military Medal – the highest honour that could be awarded to a private in the First World War. It was like so many stories form the Somme a tale of loyalty, of unimaginable strength mental and physical, of staggering courage and of utter futility.

Wogga found the fun in everything and where there was no fun to find he shut it out. For a boy who had chosen to experience the worst of man's inhumanity to man he was remarkably uncomfortable with real conflict of any kind. Perhaps it was because he had experienced the worst.

He almost always wore a suit, shoes polished daily. His principles were equally impeccable. He believed in manners, not prissy formality but genuine respect, standing up to shake hands, opening doors for others, always calling my maternal grandparents Mr and Mrs Headey. We saw the soft side; we knew he could be tough. He was loyal to the weak, harsh to the unkind. I often recall his withering contempt for the wealthy man (it always seemed to be a man) who 'wouldn't spit to give you a slide'. And he's been gone twenty years now but still I catch myself in new situations modelling my behaviour on how I imagine he might have behaved, saying the things he would have said, staying strong and silent when I know he would have been, honing my values, trying to be Wogga Robinson.

He was Robin Hood, and Muhammad Ali, super hero, Tarzan, and the funniest, happiest, naughtiest man I knew. Shortly before he died he said that I was just like him when he was my age. I remember it perfectly. We were sat alone together after breakfast at my parents' house. It was a hot August Sunday and the midday sun was streaming through the open window – meals together would last for hours. It is one of my most cherished memories. One, perhaps, that I will tell my grandchildren some day after boxing or rugby with a rolled-up sock or a balloon game at Christmas time.

David Robinson is a community worker living and working in East London. He has founded and run several organisations and social programmes including Community Links, We Are What We Do, and the Children's Discovery Centre. He now leads the Prime Minister's Council on Social Action.

Sir Stuart Rose

On the desk in my office is a black-and-white photo-graph of a good-looking man seated in a chair and surrounded by the sort of leafy green plants you associ-ate with old-fashioned colonial splendour. The only clue to his identity is that he has the same shaped nose as my father, but there are no memories attached to either the man or the setting of the picture.

This is my father's father – my grandfather – and I never met him. In fact I only acquired the photograph a few months ago and looking at the picture is a bit like finding a missing piece of a jigsaw puzzle that is still far from complete.

That jigsaw puzzle is my family history. I have no memory of either set of grandparents and though it would be an exaggeration to say this is something that has dominated my life, it is something I think about increasingly as I get older.

Without grandparents everything stops with my immediate family – of which there are now just my father, my sister and myself.

There is nothing tangible that I can grasp to under-stand more about where I came from or what my heritage is. And in a strange way, not having known my grandparents highlights what I don't know about myself as much as what I don't know about my family.

The colonial impression given by the photograph of my paternal grandfather is somewhat misleading – but his life is no less exotic-sounding. Both he and my grandmother were White Russian émigrés who fled to China after the 1917 revolution and then settled in South America – one in Argentina and one in Paraguay. My father did not go with either of his parents and was instead rescued by a Quaker spinster teacher in China, and taken to England where he was educated. As a result my father never saw his own father again, and only saw his mother once. I never met either of these grandparents.

Similarly I did not know my maternal grandparents. My mother, who was born in Egypt, had a distant relationship with her own mother, who during the 1920s can best be described as something of a social gadfly. She sounds like an incredibly interesting woman who was far ahead of her time: according to stories she used to catch turtles and ran a number of business enterprises. But pursuing these hobbies gave her little time for her own family.

Eventually she had a second family, and more children. I met her when I was in my teens and she did not show any interest in me. My mother's father died when she was just thirteen so I never met him.

Perhaps it was a blend of this sense of rootlessness on

the part of both my parents, and my mother's somewhat difficult relationship with her own mother, but my parents worked hard to ensure my sister and I had functional and stable lives. And yet, even with such a secure upbringing I feel acutely a sense of loss from not having known my grandparents.

I had a lot of unanswered questions. I wondered, for instance, whether there would ever have been an alternative place to go to for advice, or if there might have been someone who would always have had time for me without the distraction of work.

Of course it is very easy for me to romanticise the role of grandparents. But I did grow up with the sense that there was something missing – a link with the past, and with the very people who give you your roots. This has made me inquisitive about the things and the people I do not know – and as I get older this sense of curiosity becomes greater.

This was crystallised in early 2008 when my father, who is now in his eighties, said that he had one ambition left, and that was to see his father's grave. He had not seen his father since he was a teenager, more than seventy years ago.

Two months after we had that conversation I took him to Paraguay, where his father had settled. It was an emotional journey, where my father got to meet family he never knew existed and I learned a little about my own heritage.

As we came through customs at the airport I immediately recognised my father's half-sister. It was the same resemblance I had when I first the saw the photograph of my grandfather. We also met my father's nephews, nieces and my cousin in Paraguay.

The trip made me realise that there were all these people who are connected to me who are strangers. And I came away feeling that it would have been nice to have more of us when I was growing up.

So, as I sit here now, looking at the photograph of my grandfather I wonder what it would have been like to have a kindly older grandparent in my life. Of course it is a romanticised view. But not having known my grandparents has made me determined to make a real effort with my own grandchildren when they come along. I will take them on trips. I will take them to the theatre. I will teach them how to shoot.

And I, as a grandparent will have a romantic view of my grandchildren. I will be more thoughtful of putting aside quality time to spend with them. It is a bit of a conscious pay back: what you don't do for your own children you would like to be able to do for your grandchildren.

Sir Stuart Rose is Executive Chairman of Marks & Spencer. He was knighted for his services to the retail industry and corporate social responsibility.

Michael Simkins

I'm ideally qualified to know just how important grandparents are. I never had any.

Or rather, I had them once, but all four of them had passed on by the time I was born. Thus during my childhood, the notion of my own mum and dad ever having had their own equivalents was a concept beyond my understanding.

I spent time with other people's grandparents of course; at Christmas parties or weddings, or when I'd nip back to watch telly at a mate's house after school – they'd usually be silver-haired old figures who lived in an upstairs room or a granny flat, wandering in occasionally to look for their glasses while we were ensconced watching *Top of the Pops*. Yet I never really quite knew who these figures were or what they were doing, simply because I had no comparable figures in my own life.

The irony is that the older I've got, the more I've come to know my grandparents and the greater my appreciation of them. Both their features and their influence on who I am have started bleeding through, until now, at the age of fifty-one, I can both see and feel them staring back at me when I look in the mirror.

Take my paternal granddad Len, for instance. One of eight brothers (the last of which was named Octer) he was apparently a pretty dab hand at parlour entertainment in his prime, singing songs and entertaining his colleagues in the canteen at the Woolwich Arsenal where he worked during the Great War. Eventually he rose to the dizzy heights of President of the Wembley branch of the Grand Order of Water Buffaloes, a local performing group who, I imagine, sported some pretty impressive ceremonial headgear.

When his son Benny, my dad, started following his footsteps, even to the point of taking up the tenor saxophone, Len merely encouraged him rather than insisting he spend his time on more commercial pursuits as might have been expected in those more prosaic times, and thus Benny inherited the same laid-back attitude when I too announced my intention to have a go at the stage for a living.

My dad used to sing old parlour songs that he'd learned off Len: and now I sing them too if the occasion is appropriate: 'Stammering Sam', 'The Ragtime Goblin Man', and 'Jumping Johnston'. I know of nobody else who has even heard of these numbers, but to me they're a direct link back to a granddad I wish I'd known.

My maternal grandmother, Edith, I know less about, but photographs suggest a small, crisp Cornish woman, the pillar on which the garrulous tendencies of her husband could cling like a vine as he soft-shoed his way around the pubs and clubs of North London.

My maternal grandparents have influenced me even more in a way, even though they hadn't an ounce of theatrical blood in their veins. While my dad rarely mentioned his own folks, Mum's were part of her every-day conversation.

Bill and Alice Holliday lived all their lives in Cheltenham: consequently my own mum never lost her love for that lovely corner of the Cotswolds – nor her Gloucestershire dialect. Bill, a master builder, was a kindly, unmaterialistic man, always lending people the odd tenner to get them through or letting out his spare room at home for friends who'd fallen on hard times and needed somewhere to stay. Several of his houses still stand in the town today.

His business was apparently ruined by some indus-trial action by his workforce in the later 1930s, an action for which my mum blamed the Trade Unions and for which she never forgave them to her dying day. When the annual Trade Unions Congress came to our home town of Brighton, as it did every few years, Mum would delight in overcharging delegates if they were foolish enough to come in our sweetshop for some fags or a quarter of sherbet lemons: each small diddle she considered a payback for the demise of her own dad's business. Yet in all other ways she was kindly, scrupulous and fiercely forgiving; traits I've done my best to continue.

My mum loved her mother Alice with all her heart, and her death after a long battle with illness on Christmas Eve 1936 affected Peggy deeply. Thus she too was never easy with the prospect of illness after that, and spent her latter years simply refusing to acknowledge the inevitable wear and tear of getting old, blaming poor circulation or seizing joints by claiming that the recalcitrant organs were 'just playing silly devils'. Much as Alice had done fifty years earlier, I imagine.

Nowadays I see my own grandparents reflected back at me both physically and emotionally. Lenny's long nose, his delight in company and in being a bit of a show off. Or Alice's soft kindly, slightly fearful eyes. The older I get, the nearer I get to knowing them.

Nowadays, in this medically enhanced age when eighty is the new sixty, I come across kids who even spend time with even their great-grandparents. I envy them. That must be very special.

There's a Buddhist quotation that runs thus: 'If you want to know the causes you made in the past, look at the effects in your present life: and if you want to know the effects in the future, look at the causes you are making today.' As a summary of the importance of grandparents, I don't think it can be bettered.

Michael Simkins is an actor and author based in London. His second book, Fatty Batter, *was shortlisted for the 2008 Costa Book Prize and his third,* Detour De France, *was published earlier this year.*

Sam Smethers

After my mother's illness and death at the age of twenty-six when I was just seven years old, and in the absence of my dad, I was brought up by my maternal grandparents. My nan, Josie, worked part-time as a cleaner and my granddad, Stan, as a messenger (a kind of internal postman) for a company in the City. By any conventional measure of it, I had a deprived childhood. We had no car, no telephone and all our carpets and furniture was second-hand, as were most of my clothes. We never went on holiday, apart from a day trip to Southend (which I loved). But when I look back at that time I feel all the richer for it.

We used to spend hours talking together or playing games. They were always prepared to listen to me and to explain. I was never smacked and hardly ever sternly spoken to. My overriding memory is that I was loved by them unconditionally every day of my life. As I grew up I had this strong sense that they were both on my side. That feeling of support and strength hasn't left me despite the fact that they both died some years ago. It is thanks to the love, stability and security that they gave me that in turn I have been able to become a loving partner and mother myself.

I am sure that I would have been in local authority foster care if Nan and Granddad had not been there to look after me. I doubt very much that I would be able to look back on my childhood with the same feelings of warmth and positivity if that had been my experience.

It is one of the great paradoxes of life that as a society we have the ability to place so little value on something so fundamental to us. The quiet contribution that grandparents make every day usually goes unnoticed and uncelebrated, at least by the world outside. But you can bet that every day there are thousands of children who understand and value it. And there is an even greater number of adults who look back with real gratitude, as I do, for what their grandparents did for them.

Sam Smethers is Chief Executive of Grandparents Plus.

Lord Stevens

My grandfather was a character. He had been a police-man around Lambeth and Brixton for thirty years.

He didn't want promotion and when he retired from the Metropolitan police he was encouraged by others to become a local councillor. Again he refused. He went with my grandmother to live in North Wales where he became a security officer at a large factory complex near Chester. I spent many of my younger years in North Wales. On the early death of my grandmother, as a result of cancer, he went to live with my aunt at Mandrake Road, Tooting Bec. It was here that I got to know him in a more intimate sense.

I suppose I was his favourite grandchild. We discussed at length his time as a policeman; much of what he said must have had a big influence on me. He told me about being on the beat, and of the Great Strike, when he had been transferred from London to Wales to deal with strikers. He painted a picture of policing which was both humane and direct. He was not afraid to talk about laying hands on people if the need was right. He operated in an environment that was totally different from now; he was used to delivering summary judge-ment in the form of 'a clip on the ear'.

I remember him describing one instance, which disturbed him greatly, when as a pensioner he was walking past Tooting Bec Tube station when he saw two youths acting in a disorderly manner and damaging public prop-erty. He was disgusted when he saw a police officer walking on the opposite side of the street who saw what happened and ignored it. Needless to say, my grandfather took action with his walking stick. I was told by some shopkeepers that those youths are still running to this day, in the opposite direction from my grandfather. What impressed me most about him was his moral and physical bravery. He knew what was right and was determined to carry it through irrespective of the consequences. He was a man also with an immense sense of humour. The three aunts he lived with who had all seen their fiancés killed in the First World War played jokes on each other.

When the decision came that I could not continue with my career in flying, it was his influence and stories that propelled me toward the police force as a career – much against my father's better judgement at the time. My grandfather must have instilled some innate sense, for I took to policing like a duck to water – something my father later recognised.

I still have my grandfather's gold pocket watch that was presented to him when he left the Metropolitan

Police force after thirty years, which has inscribed on it: 'From your friends and colleagues in admiration'. It is something I still treasure and will pass on to my son who has followed in our footsteps with a career in the Metropolitan Police.

There is no doubt that my grandfather, having served as a police constable for thirty years deserves as much admiration and thanks than some of us who reached high rank. His was a career solely on the front line.

Lord Stevens was the Commissioner of the Metropolitan police from 2000 to 2005. He is now International Security Advisor to the Prime Minister.

Jean Stogdon

When I became a grandmother in 1981 I was a manager of two hundred staff in a busy Inner London social services department. I worked long hours and was almost unavailable as a childcare resource for my grandchildren. I felt very guilty as my grandchildren were variously cared for in day nurseries, with childminders and nannies. I questioned whether my career was more important than caring for my grandchildren while their parents worked. My mother, having brought up her three children, moved seamlessly from her role as a full-time mother to a full-time grandmother. With a great struggle I came to terms with the fact, as today's parents must, that we have choices. We live in different times.

The dilemma continues for many grandparents to this day. We have done our bit, even the double shift – many of us had to manage the work-life balance. Now we look forward to freedom from work and to a certain extent from family responsibilities. We have responsibilities to ourselves. We have thirty-odd years' extra life this century and are fitter. There are greater opportunities for older people. If one word sums up my life it is choice.

If grandparents are not what they used to be neither is the task of being a grandparent; we are in transition. Family life has changed so drastically, with working parents and the divorce rate so high. There is great diversity and ostensibly many options; it seems everyone wants to define and redefine family life. Grandparents are in the eye of the storm of change. Both my grandmother's and my mother's marriages were terminated by death; my own marriage lasted for fifty-seven years yet already one of my sons is divorced. Divorce is a family business with grandparents witnessing the painful process but being powerless to do anything but stand by and offer support.

I have been lucky. Having sons increases the risk of losing touch with or even being denied contact with our grandchildren. Fortunately my relationship with my grandchildren is valued and continues to grow, and if anything contact is even more frequent as I adopt and adapt to the role of assisting them.

There are many different issues for grandparents, depending on the circumstances of our children. Some people will become grandparents by adoption, or they may lose their grandchildren through adoption. Others will have grandchildren in lesbian or gay households and may have to come to terms with what was previously unthinkable. A few will have grandchildren subject to care proceedings because their grandchildren have been neglected or abused. Furthermore, grandchildren could have at least one parent from a different ethnic group. We may lose our grandchildren through divorce, or gain grandchildren and become step-grandparents. Our grandchildren's parents may be disabled, or the children may need special help. All these situations and many others challenge us.

Most grandparents will step in if needs must. But there is evidence that there may be ambivalence if we are asked to do too much, at a moment when we are poised to pursue our own choices and opportunities, perhaps for the first time after a life of work. But love is deep and family continuity and family preservation are vitally important to most grandmothers. Although most of our caring is invisible and unsung I believe it is the glue that holds many families together.

Jean Stogdon has three sons, Philip, Andrew and Mark and has four grandchildren, Hannah, Thomas, Grace and Molly. She is a former chair of the Grandparents' Federation, and has set up Grandparents Plus, which provides training on kinship care and ageism to people working with grandparents and extended families.

How I Learned to be a Granny
Miriam Stoppard

One of my cardinal beliefs of child rearing is 'take your lead from your baby'. This means giving your baby the space to teach you about their needs at each stage of development rather than you imposing your expectations on your baby.

As granny to eleven grandchildren I've learned that the best grandparent strategy is, once again, to take your lead from your children, only this time they are the parents. That means giving them the space to bring up their children, your grandchildren, as they think fit without you imposing your views on them, no matter how much you disapprove, even if it brings you pain.

I was quick to put my own mother straight when she disagreed with my parenting style, so I would do anything to avoid my sons and daughters-in-law telling me to butt out.

At the slightest hint of a looming disagreement my

children, thank heaven, have been quick to step in and steer me away from a possible confrontation.

The first time this happened is etched on my memory, not because I had to back painfully down, but because my son simply took charge of me and my emotions. His first daughter was three months old and I was babysitting. It went like this:

'Mum, I know you don't believe in letting babies cry, so this is going to be hard for you. And I don't like giving you orders but this is an order. We want Esmé to get used to being left in her cot and to be happy in it. So we've decided on a policy of rapid return. Please follow it.'

Rapid return means when the baby cries you wait a couple of minutes then go silently into the room, comfort the baby with a few pats and then wordlessly leave the room. No pick ups. You can repeat this as often as you like – and may have to, many times – with Esmé's first time I did rapid return with a breaking heart more than thirty times. I wasn't there for subsequent nights but Esmé required half as many returns on night two and by night four she'd learned to comfort and quiet herself.

Triumph! And a lesson learned all round, especially by me. I didn't have the courage of my son and daughter-in-law when bringing up said son, now father, to follow their firm but humane strategy and as a result my son was a wakeful child, requiring my presence in order to sleep till he reached the age of five.

This early granny experience convinced me that the most valuable (to my children) and satisfying (to me) role I could play was mother's help – taking orders or ascertaining preferences with a willing heart. To many grandparents that might feel like a downgrade, given their lifetime of experience and the fact that their care-taking often permits a standard of living their children wouldn't otherwise enjoy. But the alternative is one I can't contemplate and worth remembering by all grand-parents: your children can levy the ultimate sanction – disbarring you from seeing your grandchildren.

This is territory I won't venture into and that imper-ative informs all my behaviour. As a willing student of grandparenthood I'm given the opportunity to hone whatever skills I have every single day.

Just the other night, when my daughter-in-law was being besieged simultaneously by her three small daughters, she deftly assuaged all their needs by saying, 'Sometimes you have to share Mummy, now Maggie your turn first, then it's your turn Evie (both these twin girls are two and a half) and Esmé, because you're five now, you can have a turn after your sisters.'

Later that evening, when all three were demanding to get on my lap, I found myself echoing my daughter-in-law's sage words, saying, 'You'll just have to share Granny…' What a great lesson for us all.

Almost everything I've learned about being a granny I've learned from my children. They are so much wiser about grannyhood than I am. And that's because they maximise my strengths and usefulness and play down my weaknesses and shortcomings. They're superb managers of this particular granny and as a result it's win—win for all of us, most of all for the children in whose care I wish to share.

It's not difficult to defer to my children because I see them being more patient, more respecting of their children and more understanding than I ever was with mine. In fact it's easy to praise them on being good parents. Every time I'm with them I watch them doing things I didn't do with my own children and wish I had. I see my grandchildren responding with delight as they're encouraged, helped, shown and praised in a way that never occurred to me. Of course, now and then I think the odd thing might be done differently but why dwell on the occasional negative when there are so many positives to concentrate on?

It's a bit like marriage – there are seven things out of ten that you adore about your partner and three things out of ten that drive you crazy. But you concentrate on the seven. It's not useful or productive to do otherwise. It's the same with your children's parenting skills. There's always something you can praise. And my, doesn't it oil the wheels. All parents, including your children, are worried lest they aren't coming up to scratch so the occasional vote of confidence from you does wonders and will make you a grandparent who's welcomed and cherished.

It also makes it unlikely that you'll run your children or your grandchildren down. It seems odd to me that grandparents feel free to poormouth their children and criticise their grandchildren, but they do. Nothing is more calculated to make you an unpopular grandparent.

As a result I've become a much better granny than I was a parent. In fact, I now see that I was put on earth to be a granny. I never thought that about my parental role. As a working mum I had precious little time to reflect on what that meant whereas I realise becoming a grandparent is an opportunity to grow – and how can we not take advantage of that at our time of life?

Miriam Stoppard, M.D., DSc, FRCP, LLD, has been at the forefront of health information since she began her writing and broadcasting career in the early 1970s. She has published over 50 books and has become well-known to millions as an authority on a range of health issues. She is married to Sir Christopher Hogg and has four sons, two stepdaughters and eleven grandchildren.

Alan Titchmarsh

Mum's mum, Catherine Naylor, came from Bradford, and her dad, George Herbert Hardisty, from Skipton. Herbert was a 'ganger' – a sort of foreman – in the council's highways department. He smoked a pipe filled with rich-smelling Condor tobacco and was bald with a walrus moustache. He seemed always to be wearing dark trousers, a dark waistcoat with a watch chain, and a white collarless shirt. A flat cap (or black trilby on Sundays) covered his bald head when he was out. By the time I came along he was retired and had time to be a small child's perfect granddad, kindly, gentle and with a few tricks up his sleeve. While Granddad was short and stocky, Grandma was angular and slender-featured with swollen rheumatic knuckles. She was, of our two grandmas, the one who spoiled my sister and me the most.

Gardening is what I have done for as long as I can remember. I have a photograph of myself and Granddad Hardisty on his allotment. He is leading me, a podgy-legged one-year-old in baggy bloomers, between rows of sweet peas, among which dangle the shiny lids of Cadbury's cocoa tins, put there to frighten off the sparrows. His allotment, on the banks of the river, had a small and lopsided shed filled with tools, spilled seeds and bags of pungent fertiliser. Blackberries scrambled over brass bedsteads, and a sunken tank of sootwater provided the wherewithal to discourage greenfly, caterpillars and anything else that might want to eat his cabbages and cauliflowers, all of which seemed to be covered in a thin black film of soot. Grandma must have had to scrub each brassica for hours to remove the deposit.

In the back kitchen of the Hardisty household in Ash Grove – the other side of the Leeds Road from Dean Street and where we would visit them two or three times a week – were produced toasted currant teacakes, spread with butter that melted and ran in rivulets down our chins. Grandma had an amber sugar bowl, and Granddad would keep his empty tobacco tins and matchboxes for us, making long trains out of them and pushing them over the edge of the brown chenille-covered table to land with a clatter on the stone-flagged floor. He could make a squeaking noise with his hands – we called it 'cupty-cupty' – and, to the despair of my mother, he would drink his tea from his saucer, having poured it there from his cup to cool it down before slurping it up under the drooping grey whiskers of his moustache. Then he'd wink at us, fill his pipe and sit in his big armchair, pulled up by the fire that glowed in the massive kitchen range, shiny black with steel handles.

Sometimes, in moments of sentimentality, he would sing 'My Old Dutch' to Grandma, who would turn away and mutter 'Shut up, Herbert', wiping a tear from her eye with the corner of her pinny.

Looking back at my mum's parents, whom I knew for only eight years, I realise now how much Kitty and Herbert Hardisty taught me about love. Not effusively, just indirectly, by example. They were quite ordinary or they certainly seemed so. My granddad would go to the British Legion for a drink with my dad, and they'd play dominoes. Granddad worked at the Liberal Club in his retirement, cleaning and serving behind the bar, with a robust couple called Mr and Mrs Boyle, whom I remember smoking a lot. Grandma would occasionally snap at him 'move your feet, Herbert', but there was always a magic between them. I can recognise it now.

I have a black-and-white photo of them taken on a day trip to Hornsea on the Yorkshire coast not long before they died – Granddad in his flat cap and suit, a coat folded over his arm and Grandma, wearing a strange felt hat, the bandages showing under her stockings, her arm linked through that of my granddad. There's a tired, almost haunted look about them, as though they are on the brink of a journey into the unknown. I suppose they were.

Alan Titchmarsh is a broadcaster, gardening expert, writer and novelist.

Mother Rat

Marina Warner

When you are young, grandparents appear immeasurably old: my grandpa Plum, once a famous cricketer, seemed to have passed beyond ordinary earthlings' needs, even though remaining with us. He was so thin when I was a child that when asked how much he wanted for lunch would reply, absent-mindedly from behind his paper, 'One pea, please.' His wife, my granny, Agnes née Blyth, once a slender gin and port heiress, had become a cosy smiling Mrs Sprat, fur-wrapped and soft as a marshmallow. She was the only granny I knew, as my other one, the Italian one, my mother's mother, was living in Chicago and we didn't fly to the US in the years after the war as lightly as we do today.

My father called his mother Mother Rat, his pet name for her when he was a boy who was very fond of rats which he kept as pets; but my mother heard this nickname as 'motherette' and in my mind she became a kind of alternative to a suffragette, that is another kind of female, a motherette. Mother Rat was usually to be

found in bed, offering a toffee from the tin she kept
beside her; on the lid was a picture of a couple in fancy
dress, top hat, tails, pink bonnet and beribboned bustle
dress and parasol, looking in at a shop window with
mullioned panes at a whole display of tins in the shop
window with a picture on them of a couple in fancy
dress, top hat, tails… everyone knows this lovely puzzle
and the vertigo of infinite recession. I used to pore over
it to see the very smallest of the repeated images deep
down in the surface of the tin. After the war, my parents
gave Granny our sugar ration coupons because we'd
grown up abroad and so we hadn't acquired the same
taste for Fry's chocolates or the Quality Street assort-
ment in their colour-coded wrappers. Every afternoon,
granny used to peg her way down the corridor to use the
telephone which stood in the hall by the front door and
place bets with her bookie on the races: her daily flutter.

The reasons Mother Rat had taken to her bed were
complicated and personal: heart trouble was the official
cause, and it may have been in more ways than one.
Agnes Blyth belonged to an era when a young woman of
her class was still fettered by the polite constraints against
which Charlotte Brontë had railed and Florence
Nightingale had fought, and it did atrophy women. She
was slower and older for her age than she need have
been. Looking back, I can see she had narrowed her life
and let her energies droop at an age when women of my

generation like to think of ourselves as simply entering a slightly advanced phase of youth.

I read recently that a psychoanalyst – Enid Balint – proposed that there should be a phrase 'to be empty of oneself' by analogy with the common expression, 'to be full of oneself'. Someone who is empty of herself needs others to reassure her, to fill her up with affirmations of presence and to draw comforting boundaries around her, while at the same time offering horizons of possibility and throwing open doors. 'To be empty of oneself,' writes Balint, 'is to experience a void in the place where confirmation or acceptance of one's identity should be, confirmation of the kind that is asked for by a child when he shows his mother a cut or a graze and is told that it will "be all right".' My granny came from a world that probably didn't give her much to fill up her emptiness. But she did pour out emotional riches on me, and Enid Balint describes the exactly similar situation and I recall my own surprise at the lavishness of Mother Rat's assurances.

It was 1952 and I had fallen in Kensington Park on the tarmac by the Round Pond where I went every afternoon with my little sister, sometimes to visit Peter Pan and sometimes, if there was a breeze, to watch the toy sailboats plying the water. I'd grazed my knee and my nanny (we had an austere nanny in a uniform with a brown felt hat and a hatband and a very great love of my baby sister whom she wheeled in the pram) brushed the matter aside as nothing, so when I came in to my granny's bedroom where she was sitting propped up in her high bed with her plump satin eiderdown and her big pillows, I was astonished that she listened all ears to my tale of falling in the park, and cried out, with what seemed to me genuine anguish, 'My poor lamb! Let me kiss it better,' and then insisted on seeing the wound so that I had to raise my knee with its sad scratch, that unheroic trace of a clumsy girl's battle lost with skipping rope or ball, on to the sheets for her to examine closely and then brush her lips on my skin, in order to pronounce it well again and so leave me full – of glee, of glory, of appetite for tea.

Marina Warner is currently working on a novel, Inventory of a Life Mislaid, *and a study of Magic and the 1001 Nights. She teaches Literature at the University of Essex and lives in London.*

Perween Warsi

I still remember very clearly the very first sight of my grandma waiting at the front door to receive us with open arms full of love and affection!

My father was in a government job in India – posted a long way away from our grandparents' home. The excitement of going to see her was just incredible. That day would never come fast enough. The preparation used to start months before, or at least in my imagination it did!

I come from a large family – six uncles, aunts and dozens of cousins. We all used to gather around at least once a year for two weeks. The house was full of fun and laughter – like being in a *mela* (party/celebration). The house was (and still is) not just large but constructed in such a way that it gave each family a house within the house, while maintaining a sense of the larger family. After our grandparents had gone to sleep we used to gather in the place of one of our uncles, chatting, having tea and a midnight feast.

Talking about food; even with servants, cooking meals four times a day for thirty to fourty people (not forgetting the visitors who would just drop in) was a challenge but a great experience of how to organise an unplanned party. Other than the making of afternoon tea (which was my grandfather's job) the rest was left entirely to my grandma and rightly so. She was a great organiser, brilliant administrator and a fantastic cook. This is when I realised that cooking was not a chore but great fun – watching young and old enjoying food, licking their fingers and making mmmm sounds gives you an enormous pleasure!

Breakfast was the best meal of the day. We all used to help out in the kitchen, as it had to be served by 7 a.m. on the dot and no one should be left to last. After the evening meal grandmother would light her Hubble Bubble pipe surrounded by all her grandchildren ready to tell us a story. Her stories seemed to last for weeks. Behind every story there was always a message.

Two messages from my grandmother have always stuck with me.

Family is more important than anything else – money comes and goes; family always sticks together not just in the good times but also in bad times.

Care for others especially those who are less fortunate than you are. The pleasure should be more in giving than receiving. If we all shared our wealth nobody would be poor.

Her actions spoke louder than her words.

These two teachings have to this day stayed with our entire family and for that I am so proud.

I can already see some signs of these values in my granddaughter who is the most beautiful, loving, and adorable child in the world.

Perween Warsi was born in India and moved to the United Kingdom in 1975. Disappointed with the quality of Indian food available in the UK she set up her company, S&A Foods, from her kitchen. It now employs over 600 staff. Perween was awarded the CBE in 2002 and a CBI First Women award for lifetime achievement in 2005.

Letter to My Grandmother, Zena Roberts, Who Died in 1992

Tina Weaver

Dearest Granny,

I can picture you so vividly clapping your hands together gleefully as I paraded yet another outfit. 'Ooh that's a bobby dazzler!' you'd say when the truth was it was probably a real shocker bought on a Saturday afternoon shopping trip and crudely modified, as, aged ten, I fancied myself as a bit of a designer.

In your eyes I could do no wrong , I was never being argumentative, difficult, sloppy with my homework, or wearing too much blue sparkly eye shadow. Heavens no, I was simply 'misunderstood'. You were always there – when Mum was cross, when I was feeling down. You made me feel ten feet tall.

As I was growing up you, Granny, were my faithful guide and friend. Your 'Tommy Troubles', that's what you called me, and you always said it with a fond sigh and a smile.

I remember our moments together, just the two of us, as clearly as if we had only parted this afternoon. You lighting the fire. Me sitting at your feet. Beside us, a tray of tea, laid out with those gold-rimmed fine china cups, the pot warm beneath that hand-knitted cosy, and a very springy Victoria sponge sitting on a paper doily. Maybe hours went by, I don't know. I was just transfixed by your humbling tales, of a world before my time.

How you hid under the kitchen table for shelter in the wartime air raids because you didn't want to leave the house.

How you had to send your daughter – my mother – then aged four, off to rural Wales, an evacuee for five long years.

How you and Grandpa drove through moonlit nights to visit her, bumping along roads where head-lights weren't allowed, hoping there would be less risk of enemy raids in a full moon, determined to keep the family intact no matter what the hardships. And rather hoping you may just hit a pheasant so you could pluck it for lunch!

It was a world before pre-packed supermarket food. You even knew how to skin a rabbit at my age, while I shamefully struggle to carve a Sunday joint! Grandpa collected fresh Malvern water from a spring on the hills in an old milk urn. You helped give me a glorious idyllic childhood.

And what about your shortcake? That special recipe which to this day, despite 103 attempts, no-one in the family has managed to recreate. I can still savour its taste. Spread far too thickly with butter, of course. You were known for drenching everything in butter or double cream. Healthy eating? 'Pah!', you'd scoff. I can hear you now. 'You didn't win the war on lettuce.'

You had those essential, old-fashioned, grandmotherly skills: cooking, baking, needlework, storytelling. Once you crocheted a special gift for me…ahem, a bright pink poncho with matching hair band. Aged five, I was proud to wear it! Today I still keep it and cherish it, along with all the sweaters you so lovingly knitted.

I remember, too, later days, and the painful, gradual realisation that our relationship was changing, our roles were reversing. You were becoming the fragile, little one, in need of love and care. How cruel it seemed. In no time you were bent double, with delicate bones. Now I was your helper and guide.

Work meant I had to move from home to London, but you loved to call me in the office, two or three times a week. Your hearing wasn't too good. Very often my bemused colleagues had no choice but to listen to me on the phone, bellowing the minutiae of my life, which you insisted on receiving in detail.

'You'll be fine, my Tommy Troubles,' you would say.

I still picture you often, in my mind. When days seem

difficult, and problems insurmountable, I see my selfless, stoic, immaculate, ever-smiling, granny and I'm sure I can hear you tut-tutting at my silly self-indulgence.

Tina Weaver is editor of the Sunday Mirror *newspaper. She grew up in Malvern, Worcestershire, and her grandparents lived a mile away.*

Fay Weldon

We called her Nonna – which is Italian for grandmother. She was reluctant to be called 'gran' or 'granny' as many a smart youngish grandmother understandably is – and this was a time when grandmothers were supposed to sit by the fire and spin – chance would be a fine thing, these days! She came to live with us in Christchurch, New Zealand, in 1941, daring submarine-infested seas to do so. It was wartime. I was ten, my sister Jane twelve. Nonna had been living in fashionable San Francisco: my mother, divorced from my father, was a working single parent and Nonna was needed to help keep house for Jane and me. So she came at once.

New Zealand all those years ago was still very much a pioneering country: hard working and without frills. The living was hard. I remember the amazement with which I watched Nonna unpack her trunk. From it she drew things I did not know existed – silks and satins, little veils and Chinese wraps, delicate high-heeled shoes – we only ever wore great stompy lace ups – fancy hair combs, the *Rubaiyat of Omar Kyyam*, tissue-wrapped.

Ribbon-bound love letters. She travelled nowhere without a soft pillow for her head.

I ran ceaseless errands for her: sheet music from the library – she was a concert pianist now without concerts – detective novels likewise. She read them first, I read them when she had finished. Warships, not cargo ships, tied up in Lyttleton harbour – books were in short supply. So we too quickly got through all the green Penguins in town – Penguin paperbacks were colour-coded by subject, green was 'mystery' – and had to start again at the beginning. But most of the time Nonna played the piano – Scarlatti Variations and Mozart and a little Bach, or she sang Schubert Lieder – she'd been taught by a pupil of Clara Schumann. I don't think she did much housework but every Tuesday she made a meat loaf to the same recipe out of the remains of Sunday's roast, and every Monday early we'd light the fire in the wash-house which boiled the water in the copper for the weekly wash – and I'd come back after school and take the washing dolly to heave the dripping sheets through the ranked tubs of rinsing water to the wringer at the end of the line. I loved it.

The war ended: we returned to England; there was little luxury here either – let alone room for a proper Victorian washhouse – and Nonna went to live in comfort with my uncle Selwyn Jepson, a writer of detective novels. I think without her I'd have been a deeply and dully workaday and practical person, let alone learned that in the end you have to write the books you want to read, because no one else has written them.

Fay Weldon is a novelist, short-story writer, playwright and essayist.

Fragments From My Grandmother's Life

Lord West

Sophie Keena was my father's mother. She was born the century before last in South Wales and moved up to Hampshire as a young girl to be in service to a naval captain. I was always fascinated by the story of when she dropped the captain's alarm clock into the chamber pot and had to reimburse him slowly and painfully from her wages. She married my grandfather, a gamekeeper on the estate of Earl Montague, and had three sons. After her husband's early death, which was not unconnected with the injuries he had sustained in the First World War, Sophie moved back to Wales and married a miner. I was told he accidentally killed a man during a bare-knuckle fight, and this would make him cry after a few pints.

You will spot that my grandmother never had much of a formal education. In my boyhood in the 1950s when I would go to South Wales to stay with her, I didn't stop to wonder how intelligent she might have been. Certainly, my father was very clever but who knows where that came from? I did clock that Sophie took life on the chin and was somewhat childlike. When a Jehovah's Witness assured her that she would be reunited in heaven with her late husband, she replied 'Well, that will be a problem, see, 'cause I have two of 'em up there.'

Sophie worked in a munitions factory during the Second World War and some chemical or other made her skin and nails go yellow. She was a smoker and always resented having to forfeit her matches – a story that made my hair stand on end.

My grandmother hadn't survived without a touch of black humour. She chuckled about the day she went to visit 'old Maggie' in the local mental hospital, giving a chilling description of many doors being unlocked and fastened again in their tedious progress to Maggie's ward. 'It's very difficult to get into this place!' she had said.

'Not half as difficult as it is to get out!' replied poor Maggie.

Maggie was one of the many spinsters left high and dry from The Great War. The landscape of my grand-mother's life was not necessarily a gentle one.

I remember that Sophie was kind and uncomplicated with big strong hands and large feet and lived in a little council house that had a green chenille cloth on the dining table. Her cooking was pretty bad but I had the table to play on and the freedom to roam Barry docks, and I was happy.

My grandmother had a small insurance policy to provide for her funeral. She was always terrified of a pauper's burial. After she died and her estate was divvied up between her two surviving sons, my father was happy that she had left him just enough money to buy himself a bottle of gin and a pair of walking boots. That you could be content with not an awful lot was probably her best legacy.

Admiral the Lord West of Spithead GCB DSC DUniv served in the Royal Navy for forty-one years becoming First Sea Lord and Chief of Naval Staff. He is now a member of the Government, responsible for security and counter-terrorism.

Archbishop of Canterbury, Rowan Williams

My widowed grandmother lived with us when I was a small boy; she died when I was eight years old. Some of the most vivid memories are of Sunday evenings and the great ritual of her dressing up to go to chapel – black hat and a rather moth-eaten fur stole – which kept alive a world that, even in the 1950s, was already fading fast, the world of intense Welsh chapel devotion, strict but very deep. She symbolised all the mysterious environment of 'Ystrad', the little town (more fully, Ystradgynlais) in the Swansea valley where the family had lived before we moved to Cardiff for a while, and where we visited every few weeks: she was central in my awareness of a culture that was both strange and also profoundly my own. Like many grandparents in the mid-twentieth century she was the bridge between a world that had hardly changed for a couple of hundred years and the fast-moving post-war period. Living history.

But the memories that were most significant, I think, were of her last couple of years. It is always hard and frightening to watch someone you love dying at close quarters, especially when you're too young to understand much of what's happening. But what stayed with me was a sense of her dignity and courage. What I owe her is my first exposure to the facts of death and the possibility of facing it calmly, hopefully and without fuss – with that deep and mysterious world of devotion silently holding her through it.

Rowan Williams was born and grew up in Wales. He is a theologian, writer and poet. He was elected Archbishop of Canterbury on 23 July 2002.

The Grandmothers of Africa

Alexander McCall Smith

'So, Mma Ramotswe, what about grandmothers?'

Mma Ramotswe thought for a moment, and then smiled. 'Grandmothers, Mma? There is a lot to be said about grandmothers, and there is not all that much time.' She looked at her watch. 'No, there is not enough time to tell you all about grandmothers. That would take a long, long time. A whole day, maybe.'

'Then tell me just a few things. A few things would be quite enough.'

She settled herself into her chair. 'Very well. Grandmothers. These are ladies who are old. You do not always tell that they are old, because some of them are old ladies trying to be young ladies – you know how some people are. They think that it is good to be young and so they wear young clothes and try to walk like a young person, but they fool nobody, you know. People see them and say: *that person is an old person pretending to be a young person – it is very funny.*

'Mind you, I know why these ladies pretend not to be grandmothers. That is because of men. Some men are very good at being grandfathers – they behave as a grandfather should and they say very wise things. When those men speak, then everybody nods their heads – like this. They nod and say things like, *That is very true – what you have said, Rra, is very true. Just like the Bible.* And this encourages those old men to say more things, even if they are not all true, but sound as if they are full of wisdom. That is a very well-known problem with old men, and not just with old men, Mma.

'Now it is because of these men that ladies who are grandmothers sometimes pretend not to be grandmothers. They know that men will not look at ladies who are getting older, and so they think that the only way they can get men to look at them is to pretend to be young. The problem is that when men look at ladies like that men think: *That grandmother there is trying to look like a young girl. That is very silly, and I am not going to look at her and encourage her.* So those poor ladies get very few glances from men, no matter how hard they try; all they get is looks of pity from other women who think, *that grandmother over there should not try to be like young and glamorous women – such as ourselves; better to be a proper grandmother.*

'So you see that it is very complicated. But I do not want to waste any more of your time with those foolish people who do not want others to think that they are grandmothers. I would like to talk about real grand-mothers, and all the good things that they do.

'Things have changed, you see. There was a time when a grandmother could sit on a chair under a tree and look out over the fields and think. Or she could stay at home and sweep the yard or make sure that the mud plaster on the walls had neat patterns on it – there were many things that grandmothers could do in those days.

'They knew a lot, of course. They could tell you about how they had coped in bad times, when the rains failed and the earth was hard and dry and dusty. They knew all about how to make a little food go a long way, about how to make sure that every child was given a share no matter how empty the pots. They knew many other things too, that they could pass on.

'They also knew stories. Every child remembered stories that the grandmothers told – the stories of strange creatures and talking animals, of clever baboons who lived in caves, and leopards who had special ways of walk-ing through the darkness. And we would lie there and listen to our grandmother's voice in the night and then we would dream about the things she told us. The world of our dreams is full of strange creatures, even stranger than the creatures of a grandmother's stories.

'But then a terrible thing happened. It is not easy for us to talk about this, but I can tell you now, since you are asking me. You will know all about this, about how a sickness came, this terrible sickness, this AIDS, and how it crept across the land, suddenly, so suddenly, and laid its cold hand on almost every family, taking one here, two there, and sometimes everyone. People said that this could not last, that this illness would go away, as other illnesses went away, but it did not. People grew thin. They could not eat their food, or, if they managed to get it past their lips they could not keep it down. We were frightened – we were all frightened.

'The grandmothers were not ill, of course, because they did not have husbands any more who could pass the illness on to them. So they had to watch the family getting smaller and smaller. The father died and then the mother, and after that who was there to look after the children? The grandmother.

'So, throughout the country, the grandmothers became mothers again. Old, old ladies, who might have been sitting under those trees or walking slowly with the sun on their faces, were now looking after three, four, five children. I knew one lady who was over seventy, and she was looking after fourteen children. All had lost their mother, and the fathers had gone away or had died.

'They did not turn round and say, *Is there anyone else to look after these children?* They did not do that, because they knew that there was nobody else, and that the children needed them. And they were grandmothers, and they knew that the grandmothers of Africa would never turn round and ask another person to do this work for them. They would not do that.

'And do you know what, Mma? You know what? I have not heard any of these grandmothers – not one single one – complain about this and say that the government should be doing this or that, or how are we going to buy food if we have no money? They have not said that. They have simply looked after the children as best they could.

'I hope this will end one day, Mma. Perhaps it will. They have drugs now that are helping to stop this sickness that is cutting, cutting at Africa. But in the meantime, the grandmothers must do this thing.

'They are very tired, and one day I know that they will become late and they will be taken up into that place which is up there, that place that is like our country but is not our country. They will be taken there and there will be waiting for them, the late parents and the late children, and they will welcome the grandmother with much singing. And there will be white cattle – the sweet-breathed white cattle who live there – and they will lead the late grandmothers to a special place where there is sun and where they can sit under a tree and rest. And the children will bring them food, and flowers, and water for their thirst, to thank them for all that they have done when they were grandmothers.

'I hope that will happen. I think it will.'

Alexander McCall Smith is the author of over sixty books on a wide array of subjects. He is best known for his award-winning No. 1 Ladies' Detective Agency *series, set in Botswana, which has been translated into forty-five languages.*

Further Information

Action on Elder Abuse (AEA) works to protect and prevent the abuse of vulnerable older adults. They are the only charity in the UK and Ireland working exclusively on the issue today. www.elderabuse.org.uk 0808 808 8141

Age Concern and Help the Aged is dedicated to improving the lives of older people. It provides information and advice and other direct services to older people, influences public policy on their behalf, helps improve the perception of older people in society and celebrates the positives of growing older. www.ageconcern.org.uk   0800 00 99 66
www.helptheaged.org.uk   020 7278 1114

Grandparents Plus is the national charity which champions the vital role of grandparents and the wider family in children's lives – especially when they take on a caring role in difficult family circumstances.
www.grandparentsplus.org.uk 020 8981 8001

The Grandparents' Association is currently the only national registered charity working for children on contact and residence issues in public and private law. They give practical advice and information on issues such as welfare benefit advice for full time carers, grandparent and toddlers groups and kinship care support.
Helpline: 0845 4339585
www.grandparents-association.org.uk

PiggyBankKids is about changing children's lives. Every single child is precious and unique. At PiggyBankKids we work hard to give children the best possible chance of living a healthy and happy life, here in the UK. We want to help as many children as we can: from the vulnerable babies whose lives could be saved with the right scientific breakthroughs, to those kids and young people who have the hardest start in life.

The charity was founded by Sarah Brown in 2002 to help inspiring professionals continue their world-changing work in saving and transforming children's lives.

Jennifer Brown Research Laboratory

The researchers at the groundbreaking Jennifer Brown Research Laboratory are doing just that; working to solve some of the most devastating pregnancy problems and find better ways to look after premature babies. Supported by the Jennifer Brown Research Fund, our talented and dedicated team of doctors, scientists and research midwives are advancing pioneering research projects. Their aim is to make real progress towards resolving some of the life-threatening complications that can arise during pregnancy for both mums and babies. The work in the laboratory furthers understanding of what causes early labour, how we can develop treatments to prevent it, and how we can better help treasured tiny newborns in those first crucial hours and days after birth.

The Jennifer Brown Research Fund

The Jennifer Brown Research Fund also supports small innovative community-based schemes led by nurses and midwives. Recent programmes like the Jennifer Brown Fife Appeal encourage local health professionals to seek funding for their own community health projects. One great idea is Granny School: a refresher course for the first time grandparents who provide so much informal care and support as their grandchildren grow. This has been overwhelmed with applicants and we can see its potential for all areas across the UK. So we are funding some research to expand on how it works and inviting interest to extend pilot schemes to new areas. Other schemes generated on the ground include innovative play schemes, an antenatal care plan for mums with learning disabilities and a community research project on postnatal depression; all great ideas that are making a real difference for families that need them most.

Partnership Projects

We know that real change only comes from the passion and talents of people. That's why we work with some of the best charity leaders in the UK: heroes engaging in some of the most innovative work to help children and young adults otherwise at risk. We can support and enhance their expertise with our advice and through our Small Grants programme. PiggyBankKids gives grants that can be used for core funds – usually the hardest to fundraise for – leaving skilled voluntary sector leaders extra time to do the hands-on work they most want to do. From mentoring programmes to sports provision, children's cancer care to school-based projects, we can make a little from you go a very long way for children. In 2009 we are bringing all our Small Grants recipients together for a training day to help them thrive in tough economic times.

Chance UK

At PiggyBankKids we are passionate about mentoring, and Chance UK is one of our favourite charities transforming vulnerable children's lives. Chance UK seeks to provide an early intervention by providing targeted solution-focused mentoring for children aged five to eleven, based on their individual needs. Back in 2002 when we started, we published *Moving on Up*, a collection of well known people writing about the mentors who had most influenced their lives – including teachers. A generous grant from one of our Trustees meant that Moving on Up is now in the library of every state and independent secondary school in the UK.

Special Olympics

Our books support lots of our charity work. The international Special Olympics movement is dedicated to empowering individuals with intellectual disabilities to become physically fit, productive and respected members of society through sports training and competition. In 2005 we published *Journey to the Sea*, a collection of new fiction travel, to support the work of Special Olympics Great Britain.

For further information please contact:
Victoria Keene
PiggyBankKids
The Broadgate Tower
Third Floor
20 Primrose Street
London EC2A 2RS
020 3116 2735
www.piggybankkids.org